Floyd, Lance, and I Bike Cross-Country

Nine Weeks Across America

By

Richard Palzewic

ISBN: 1-4033-5920-2 (e-book)
ISBN: 1-4033-5921-0 (Paperback)

Library of Congress Control Number: 2002093561

This book is printed on acid free paper.

Printed in the United States of America
Bloomington, IN

To arrange speaking arrangements, contact:
Richard Palzewic
W5886 No. 14 Lane
Wallace, MI 49893
palzewic@hotmail.com

1stBooks – rev. 12/31/02

Contents

This Book is for v

Introduction.. vi

Realizing a Dream 1

Weighing Your Options... 2

Cycle America 3

Getting Ready 6

The Journey Begins 10

Northwest Sampler 12

Mission: Montana 37

Range Ride... 59

Monumental Memories.. 77

Mighty Rivers 103

Heartland Patchwork 123

Thundering Falls Spectacular 135

Empire Strikes Back 152

History Maker 167

The Day After 182

The Aftermath... 183

Life After the Trip 184

The Final Stats 187

Epilogue.. 189

Index 191

THIS BOOK IS FOR:

My parents, Barb and Larry, who raised me, showed me right from wrong, and gave me the confidence to succeed.

My six sisters, who made growing up always an adventure.

Jan.

Kathy.

Lara.

Jessy.

Julie.

Joy.

My brothers-in-law.

My nieces and nephews.

My Grandma, Katherine.

My future wife…whoever that may be.

Marcia.

Tom, who gave me support when I needed it.

Everyone who emailed me on the trip.

Cycle America.

The riders on my coast-to-coast trip…they'll remain in my mind forever.

Lance Armstrong.

Jersey Joe.

Bobby Kennedy.

Beth and Floyd Clark.

Sprocket.

Spokey.

Roxy.

Martin.

Bud.

My training partners.

The cities of Wallace, Michigan, and Rhinelander, Wisconsin.

Natasha and Bruce Smith, whose honest opinions helped me write this book.

Debra Kakuk, whose expertise at editing was greatly appreciated.

Everyone who has dreams.

Everyone who believed in me.

Everyone who didn't believe in me.

Introduction

In the summer of 2000, I participated in a coast-to-coast bicycle ride that took me from Everett, Washington, to Gloucester, Massachusetts. It was 4,300 miles and took nine weeks to complete.

What follows is a candid, no-frills, day-by-day recap of my incredible journey. It includes information on how to get started, historical information of the areas I rode through, bicycle safety and tips, general bicycle talk, pro-cycling information, advice on fitness, and funny stories and events from the summer.

This book is not meant for the expert cyclist or a Tour de France rider; it's meant for the average person or cyclist who wants to travel across the country with me.

I want you to take a different perspective when reading this book: I want you to put yourself in my shoes, and live vicariously through me so you can see the country from the seat of a bicycle; I want you to feel the sore muscles, the sweat, and the fatigue; I want you to feel the heat and cold, the rain, and the exhilaration of going 50 mph; I want you to be there with me as I ride my bike seven hours into a 25-mph headwind; I want you to see the beauty of our land and consume 6,000 calories a day; I want you to make new friends, ride up a mountain pass, and change a flat tire; last but not least, I want you to get lonely, so you can experience what I did to the fullest. If you can do all this, then you'll travel with me on my coast-to-coast adventure.

<u>Realizing a Dream</u>

When I bought my first racing bike ten years ago, it was simply to get in shape and lose some weight. As I began riding more, I saw my fitness level increase. What started out as a hobby became an obsession, as I was soon riding 150-200 miles a week, entering tours and races, and still I wanted more.

In June of 1999 I signed up for a century (a 100-mile ride) in Michigan near my parents' house. I had done the ride several times in the past, but that year's route was especially challenging. It was not only the first time I rode 100 miles in a day, but it was also unbearably hot.

After I finished the ride, I was totally whipped. I remember telling one of my sisters that there was no way I could attempt the cross-country ride that I had been contemplating for quite some time.

In July of that same summer, a couple of friends from school invited me to ride across Iowa in a bicycle tour (RAGBRAI). I figured this would be a good challenge and give me a true test of whether I could attempt a longer ride. Although extremely difficult, I managed to finish the ride in good shape. After the week-long 560-mile jaunt through the cornfields of Iowa, I realized my dream was about to come true.

Later that summer I signed up for the Coast-to-Coast 2000 Bicycle Challenge. There was definitely a strange sensation in my body as I signed my name to the waiver form and dropped it into the mail.

Fifty-one other riders from across the United States and Europe also challenged themselves to riding their bikes across the continent.

<u>Weighing Your Options</u>

If you're interested in doing long-distance cycling, the first thing you need to decide is what type of cycling you want to do. A cyclist can choose to go self-contained, or through a touring company.

Going self-contained is where a cyclist carries all their gear on the bike, and is responsible for everything while they're on the road, including food, water, sleeping arrangements, finding your own route, and mechanical breakdowns. A touring company allows a cyclist to concentrate fully on cycling, as most of the arrangements are made months in advance.

Each option also requires different equipment. A self-contained cyclist has a stronger bike, built for durability and comfort, as compared to speed. Choosing a touring company allows a biker to use a traditional road or touring bike, so they leave all their gear (except the essentials) on the luggage truck.

After weighing my options, I chose to go through a touring company. Since I didn't have any of the right equipment for solo, long-distance cycling, I knew it wasn't in my best interest to go alone. Some cyclists like that challenge, but I'm not one of them. I didn't want to have to worry about sleeping arrangements, mechanical breakdowns, food and water, and finding my own route. All I wanted to do was ride my bike.

I began searching the Internet and bicycling magazines for a tour that would fit into my summer schedule. It was a rather difficult task because many of them started before I was done teaching for the year. I finally found a tour that fit into my schedule, and settled on a company from Minnesota named Cycle America. They've been in business for decades, so I knew they were a reputable outfit.

<u>Cycle America</u>

Greg Walsh owns Cycle America, and he has a dozen or so employees who help him organize and complete his tours throughout the year. If you're not up for a cross-country tour, the company conducts several other smaller tours around the country, but their main focus is on their annual Coast-to-Coast Challenge.

The Coast-to-Coast Challenge is run in nine separate week-long segments. You can participate in as many segments as you want, but if you complete all nine, you go coast-to-coast.

The cost of the trip (when I went) was $4,500. Many people I've talked to cringe when they find out how much I paid to ride my bike across the country, but I thought it was a "steal."

The fee includes luggage transportation on a daily basis, most meals, mechanical and ride support, sleeping arrangements, a marked route, and most importantly, the chance to see the country from the seat of your bicycle.

Cycle America rents a big truck that carries your gear from town to town. Most of the meals are buffet style and the sleeping arrangements are usually inside school gymnasiums, but there is some camping as well. The company hires a route manager to ride the route in a car the day before each ride, and mark it with yellow arrows so each rider knows where to turn. There is also a mechanic who travels with Cycle America during the summer who is available throughout the day. If you happen to need any mechanical assistance, there is an added fee. The company also gives ride support throughout the day, just in case you need a lift to the next town. Finally, Cycle America hires a massage therapist to travel with the group as well (again, for an added fee).

The price does not include transportation to and from the beginning and ending of the tour, money for souvenirs, national park and ferry boat fees, and money for any other miscellaneous items that may come up (extra food, postage stamps, calling cards, etc.). There are a few hidden costs, but nothing out of the ordinary. In total, I paid about $6,000 for the entire trip.

On a typical day, you can expect to rise at 5:30 a.m. to clean up your "camp" area and get ready for the day. Breakfast is usually served at 6:30, and after looking at your cue sheet (A cue sheet is a route map that Cycle America puts together daily to point you in the right direction and give tips on things to see. I have all of my cue sheets saved, and hope to ride my coast-to-coast route in a car someday.), you are free to travel at your own pace to the next destination, typically about 80 miles away. About halfway through the day's ride, Cycle America sets up their lunch spot at the most convenient location for you to fuel-up for the remaining part of the ride. After stopping in various towns and attractions, you can expect to be done riding by the early afternoon (sometimes earlier or later, depending on the distance, weather, and scenery). After setting up your camp, a hot shower is offered, and then you'll be free to do whatever you please. I always had the same routine every day (I'll explain that later). Supper is usually served at about 5:30 p.m., and then a nightly meeting is offered to inform you about the next day's ride. Although they aren't mandatory, it's a good idea for most people to attend them. Many riders rely on the meetings to plan their next day's ride, but I on the other hand didn't take them too seriously. If I was around and felt like attending, I did, but I didn't change my plans to attend them.

You will find many different types of riders on such a tour. Many people (like myself) get up very early, ride at a reasonable pace, stop when they want to, and get to the next town. Others rise later and seem to be in slow motion, but they still manage to get to the next town before dusk. Although there really isn't a set time to begin and end the day, it's a good idea to stay somewhat with the group. Upon completion of the day, all riders need to check in with the company so they know you didn't get lost, injured, or even killed.

If you do get lost or injured on a Cycle America tour, it's very simple to contact the company and get back on track. If you can't flag down or find the company vans traveling back and forth along the route, there is a toll-free number to call. Cycle America will come pick you up or give you other specific instructions on what to do. Many riders carry cell phones with them.

A rider has several options when riding as well. One can choose to ride alone (like I did 80 percent of the time), or with others. Most people do a combination of both, but the majority ride with other people. I chose to ride alone so I could ride at my own pace, stop when I wanted to, and not have to worry about pleasing someone else. In retrospect, I wish I had ridden with more people. It would have given me a better opportunity to learn more about them.

The tour is extremely well organized. Although I've never had the opportunity to experience another tour company, many people on this cross-country trip have, and they wouldn't go with anyone else. I know if I ever do another such trip, I'll go through Cycle America. Greg Walsh told me that it takes Cycle America six months to prepare for these nine weeks of riding.

<u>Getting Ready</u>

The only way you are going to get anywhere in life is to work hard at it. There is no getting around it. If you do, you'll be a success…if you don't, you won't. Ninety-nine percent of all failures come from people who are in the habit of making excuses. I wasn't going to be one of those people.

I totally committed myself to reaching my goal of riding my bike across the country. I knew it would be difficult, but I was succeeding in overcoming life's most important fear…the fear of trying. I was very afraid, but the only way to overcome fear is to prepare yourself to the best of your ability.

Fear is something you have to learn to control and use to better yourself, because all human beings have it. The difference is how you let fear affect you. You have to be confident.

Physically and mentally, my coast-to-coast trip was the most difficult thing I've ever attempted.

The biggest mistake a person can make is to go into such an adventure ill-prepared. If you don't prepare yourself to the best of your ability, you'll find yourself sick, not riding every day, over-fatigued, and not enjoying yourself. There were people on Coast-to-Coast 2000 who were attempting the "crossing" with only a couple of hundred miles in their legs. Those were the people who didn't enjoy themselves, got sick, or couldn't ride every day. It took me a whole year of planning and training to prepare for this trip.

It's important to set your goals and ask yourself why you're doing such a trip before you go on it. I initially signed up for the physical challenge and to increase my level of fitness, but soon realized that other things were more important, like the people, their stories, and the beauty of the land.

Don't get caught up in the emotions, either. When I signed up for Coast-to-Coast 2000, I felt I could conquer the world, but as the day got nearer, I realized it would be a lot tougher than I thought. If you're riding your bike cross-country, realize the enormity of what you're doing, and that it won't be easy. It's very difficult to turn back and quit once you've begun.

Realize that such a trip will be more mental than physical. Physically you will make it if you put your mind to it, but mentally it will wear you down. After a few weeks, riding 80 miles a day is no problem physically, but knowing you *have* to is the hard part. In most cases, you'll go ten weeks without seeing anyone you know, get lonely, and miss your family. It will become like a job. In order to successfully complete a cross-country trip, your mental traits need to be stronger than your physical ones.

Also, don't do such a trip to become famous or well-known, because it won't happen. You'll more than likely get some press upon completion of your journey, but it won't be as much as you think. I was amazed at how quickly people forgot (not that it mattered) about my cross-country challenge. I was anticipating speaking to various groups about the trip, but I only got a few offers to do so. It's not uncommon for me to go three or four months and not have anyone ask me about it.

As for training miles, I'm not going to preach and harp to you that you have to ride a certain amount of miles in order to complete a long bike trip, because in all reality, anyone can do it; it all depends on your lifestyle and goals. I barely have any responsibility in my life, so I can ride when I want, and for as long as I want. I know it's not as easy for other people, so you need to focus on quality training miles.

Like any endurance sport, being a good cyclist takes many hours and years to be become really strong. Being good at cycling doesn't happen because you train hard one year. During the beginning stages of your cycling development, the physical portion is the most important. Later on you will learn mental concentration to maintain your physical strength.

When training for a multi-week bike trip, your training should target the type of riding you'll be doing during your trip. In this case, it meant riding long, slow-distance training miles. There was no need for me to be fast for the trip, so I didn't focus on gaining speed during my training.

When you train smart, you become a better rider. You have to push yourself…that's what makes the top riders. Some people can't do it, but that's what separates the good ones and the great ones.

If you look at other successful athletes, they do specific things to improve their game. Basketball players practice their shot, swimmers practice with wooden paddles on their hands, and baseball players take swings in the cage. Too many cyclists just ride their bikes and don't have a purpose when training.

Don't go into a ride thinking you'll ride yourself into shape. Although you'll see your fitness level dramatically increase, it's too risky to rely solely on this tactic. If you suddenly increase your mileage during a tour, there's a good chance that you'll get very sore and possibly pull or tear muscles. Since most cross-country tours start early in the summer, it's **extremely** important to be conditioned before the start. This includes staying active during the winter months preceding your tour.

My winter training included cross-country skiing, running, snow shoeing, and biking, both indoors and out. The winter before Coast-to-Coast 2000, I began a very strenuous eating and exercise program, and I dropped about ten pounds of fat. It was also a very mild winter, so I was biking outside by mid-February. I feel like I was able to successfully complete my cross-country tour because I worked so hard during that winter.

I was super-motivated for my tour, so training was no problem for me. I would often rise at 5:00 a.m., ride for 40-60 minutes on an indoor trainer, and then cross-country ski after school. I don't think I could have prepared myself any better.

Even though I've put 50,000 miles on my bike in the last ten years, I wasn't completely sure how much to train for a nine-week tour. I ended up putting on about 8,000 miles the year before I left, and that was more than enough. Although it's possible to complete such a tour with far fewer miles in your legs (as was evident by riders on Coast-to-Coast 2000), the more time you put into it, the more successful you'll be. For most people, a few thousand miles of training should do the trick. If you can ride 40-60 miles every day for a week, you can do a multi-week tour.

Jeff Bucher from Arizona completed the first two weeks of Coast-to-Coast 2000, and then left for Aruba (an island off the northern coast of South America) for the next five weeks. He surprised us all by showing up for the last two weeks of the tour to finish with us.

When he came back, his bike was still in the box it had been in for the last five weeks…still taped up! In other words, Jeff didn't do one mile of training during those five weeks that he wasn't on the tour! Although Jeff made it just fine, I do not recommend this.

The weather won't always be perfect, either, so it's a good idea to train in all types of weather in order to prepare yourself. Expect to ride in pouring rain, snow, and hail. Be prepared to endure drastic temperature changes, and headwinds. Since I had trained in all types of weather, I felt I had a leg up on most of the other riders, not only physically, but mentally as well. You'll find that the hardest part about training in bad weather is actually getting yourself out on the road.

Your first long-distance bike tour should not be a cross-country one. It's a good idea to work up to your goal. Start by doing single-day events, and eventually work up to week-long tours. If you can do a week-long tour, I think a multi-week tour is possible. After completing a multi-week tour, a cross-country trip may be in your grasp.

There are plenty of resources out there to help find a training program for you. Take advantage of periodicals (Bicycling Magazine) and the Internet to find a program that fits your needs.

<u>The Journey Begins</u>

I am one of the least spontaneous persons I know, so when I decided to go on this ride, there were many people who thought I was completely nuts. I not only wanted to complete the tour, but I wanted to ride every mile. A part of me said that if I didn't ride every mile, I wouldn't go coast to coast.

My good buddy, Tom Kaeser, from Marinette, Wisconsin, said to me, "Why would you want to do that? I've driven my car over the mountains out West and that was hard. That's why they invented the automobile."

Aside from the razzing that Tom gave me, he also said that I was doing a "good thing."

It was a very lonely feeling leaving Rhinelander, Wisconsin, and my home that June day in 2000. I was leaving behind security, something that I wouldn't have on the road. I made sure I rode through town to take a good look at everything, as I wouldn't see it again for the next 11 weeks. If anything happened to me along the way, I wanted to remember it in a positive way.

On June 15, 2000, my parents, my bike, and I left Michigan and went to Milwaukee, Wisconsin, to catch the Amtrak train (a first for me) out to Washington. Although it was hard to say goodbye, I knew I was about to embark on a life-long journey. I had plenty of time to think as the trip took nearly 36 hours.

Arriving in Everett, I felt very alone. What could I do? I walked into a school that was nearly abandoned and dark inside. I did find one person, another rider who was taking a nap on the gym floor. I was in a strange place halfway across the country. Alone.

It didn't take long before other riders began to show up. Being only 27, I was surprised at the ages of many riders. Most were in their 50s or 60s. I guess I was anticipating a much younger group. Looking back on the situation, I shouldn't have been so surprised. What type of person can take ten weeks off work to ride their bike 4,300 miles…retired ones or school teachers. I really had doubts about how some of them could make it, though.

We had our first meeting on the evening before the first day's ride, where we all had to introduce ourselves. It was a good chance for us to get to know each other and to hear other people's fears. I still laugh when I think back to that first meeting at how nervous everyone looked.

Our first night's camping was inside a gymnasium. Understandably, I didn't get much sleep.

Reality would set in the next morning.

Richard Palzewic

Northwest Sampler
Washington/Idaho/Montana

<u>Dipping in the Pacific</u>

Date: June 18, day 1
Start: Everett, WA
End: Skykomish, WA
Riding time: 4:20
Miles: 66
Maximum speed: 35 mph
Average speed: 15.2 mph
Elevation gain: 2,760 feet
Weather: Overcast, rainy, and cool, with temperatures in the 50s.

Did it have to rain on the first day?

Riders who left their bags outside overnight noticed they had been searched. A few items were even stolen. It was a good wake-up call as I realized security would be a big concern.

On the morning of the first ride, Cycle America set up a ceremony by the Pacific Ocean to begin the tour by dipping our tires. The idea was to dip your back tire in the Pacific, then ride across the country to dip your front tire in the Atlantic. It was a way of connecting the continent (an unusual one, at that).

With its close proximity to the ocean, the Seattle area gets a lot of rain, and this day was no exception. It was pouring rain, and my ride-every-mile attitude was put to an immediate test as I almost developed hypothermia. It wasn't what I envisioned as being the first day of my adventure.

After leaving the ceremony, a group of riders ran into immediate trouble. Only a few minutes into the ride, we ran into an expansion joint on a bridge running at a 45-degree angle. Jeff Bucher from Arizona hit the joint and crashed hard. There was a big pileup behind him and he actually had his head ridden over by another cyclist. Jeff's helmet was in five different pieces! Six other people crashed at the same spot. Since I was ahead of the action at that point, I never heard a thing, and continued on. Cycle America stopped at the scene and gave Jeff a ride to the next town. Fortunately, he wasn't badly hurt.

The incident showed the importance of wearing a helmet. Although sometimes uncomfortable to wear, I always wear one. Cycle America and most other touring companies make helmet use mandatory. You'll often see professional riders not wearing helmets. They claim they're cumbersome and add unnecessary weight. Since a lot of helmets are not very "stylish," I think a lot of riders don't wear them because they're more concerned at how they look, than being safe. I am simply amazed at how many people ***don't*** wear them. Some states make it mandatory, but the majority don't. Ninety percent of all head injuries could have been prevented if the "victim" had been wearing a helmet.

When you're braking in the rain or anytime your rims are wet, remember that the first few wheel revolutions will only dry the rim and pads, so allow yourself more stopping distance. Once "squeegeed dry," the brakes may suddenly take hold, so be ready to loosen your grip on the levers as soon as you feel the grab, or you could skid and crash.

I managed to get some arm and leg warmers at lunch from a couple other riders to help me finish. It was a day that I really just wanted to get over with. Imagine that…the first day and I didn't want to ride.

Having a destination was the best part of each day. I get bored riding on the same roads all the time, but with each pedal stroke on this trip, I was riding on roads not yet traveled upon.

Ed Collins from Minnesota, who cycled with me on Coast-to-Coast 2000, also did Coast-to-Coast 2001. When I asked him why he'd want to do the same route over again, he said he did it so he knew what to expect each day. I can respect that, but if I ever do another crossing, it will be a totally different route.

Skykomish, Washington, was our first destination.

People exploring the Cascade Mountain passes had traveled Skykomish for centuries. The coming of the Great Northern Railroad had a lot to do with it becoming a permanent settlement.

Skykomish is still a passageway for the railroad, but survives mainly because of the ski area on Stevens Pass. Stevens Pass got its name from John F. Stevens who was the chief locating engineer for the Great Northern Railroad.

When I finished the day's ride, I met a couple residents in the local diner. When I inquired about email, a young man named Johnny told me I could use his computer if I came back at 7:00 p.m. that night. Later, when I returned, he took me up to his apartment. Looking back, this probably wasn't a very smart thing to do on my part. I didn't even know the guy, and here I was in his apartment. Johnny's biggest complaint was, "there was only three good-looking ladies in the whole town."

One of the emails I received was from Don Murwin, a dentist from Menominee, Michigan. He is a personal friend of my parents, and the father-in-law of a professional cyclist named Marty Jemison.

Doctor Murwin had scanned a picture of his daughter, Marty, and himself at the 2000 United States Pro-Cycling Championships in Philadelphia (a race Marty won in 1999), and was kind enough to send it to me. Every time I felt down and depressed throughout the summer, the picture lifted my spirits and gave me added motivation.

Some time after finishing the tour, I received a package in the mail from Marty himself. Inside, were a Postal Service Jersey, and two signed posters. The jersey meant so much to me that I had it framed and hung in my classroom.

It was also in Skykomish that I found out how hard it would be to get a decent night's sleep. There was always something going on in the middle of the night that made it difficult. I remember roaming the school this night to find a secluded spot, but it seemed that wherever I went, I couldn't fall asleep. I heard a lot of trains pass through as well as a lot of snoring. I should have brought a pair of earplugs!

<u>Stevens Pass</u>

Date: June 19, day 2
Start: Skykomish, WA
End: Wenatchee, WA
Riding time: 4:50
Miles: 81
Maximum speed: 42 mph
Average speed: 16.8 mph
Elevation gain: 5,020 feet
Weather: Overcast skies, giving way to sunny conditions, with temperatures in the 80s.

I learned how hard it is to climb a mountain on a bicycle.

I had never climbed a mountain pass before, so this was an exciting day. Leaving Skykomish, I began the 16-mile climb to the top of Stevens Pass.

"That's why they invented the automobile."

I've always been a big fan of the Tour de France (a three-week, 2,300-mile race run annually in France), especially the mountain portion of the race. The mountains separate the average rider from the exceptional ones. On this day, I imagined myself in the Tour climbing L'Alpe d' Huez, a famous pass in France.

After 90 minutes of riding, I reached the summit of Stevens Pass at 4,061 feet. It would have been a beautiful ride, but much of the view was obscured due to fog. Make sure that if you ever go up the pass from the west, you stop at Deception Falls. It's a beautiful waterfall about halfway up the climb located on U.S. Highway 2.

Since aerodynamics is less important when climbing, it's important to sit up as straight as possible to open your lungs up. This will allow for easier breathing. I often put my hands on top of the handlebars, as compared to the drops. You'll see most pro cyclists doing the same thing. I try to keep as still as possible with my upper body, too, as to not waste energy (although sometimes it's impossible to do this).

On the climb, I found my fitness to be exceptional. As other riders struggled to get to the top, I "sped" (10 mph) to the summit in nearly half the time as most.

At the previous night's meeting, Greg Walsh had instructed us on how to ride ***down*** a mountain pass. Non-cyclists take it for granted as being easy to do, but it really isn't. The danger comes from using your brakes too much. Braking excessively can cause your rims to heat up which can cause a tire to blow. You can solve this dilemma by feathering your brakes, alternating between the front and back. This allows your rims to cool somewhat between applications. Another way to deal with this problem is not to use your brakes!

Speed can be another problem. I used to think going 35 mph downhill was fast (and it is), but I learned a new meaning of the word on this trip. Although my top speed going down Stevens was "only" 42, that was fast enough. (It's not uncommon for Tour de France riders to descend at over 60 mph!) If you feel as though you're going too fast, you probably are, so sit up in your saddle to increase wind drag. This will decrease your speed by as much as 10 mph.

I thought I knew what fear was, until I rode down Stevens Pass. I had overcome the fear of signing up for the tour a year ago, and leaving my home for 11 weeks; I'd overcome the fear of taking the Amtrak train for the first time and meeting new people. These fears all seemed insignificant now. I was deathly afraid of going that fast, because I knew I could actually die if I crashed.

When descending, you have to stay as composed as possible. If you think you are going to fall, it will happen, therefore, you must anticipate problems. Many riders know that if they can't beat their opponents going uphill, they have to find a way to beat them on the way down, so technique is of the utmost importance.

I took a lot of pictures on the trip, so after a photo at the summit, I began the descent. As I plunged into the clouds, I noticed how quickly the weather changed. In a matter of 20 miles, the greenness slowly vanished and the temperature began to rise. In geography terms, the eastern side of the pass was in the rain shadow (the side protected from rain-bearing winds). The clouds forming on the western side of the Cascades dump all their moisture there, so when the clouds get to the eastern part, there is very little moisture left in them. This causes drier and warmer conditions. After a chilly 41 degrees at the top of the pass, I rode in 85-degree temperature the remainder of the day.

Passing through Leavenworth, Washington, was another highlight. Forty years ago, the town relied heavily on the logging industry. Slowly, as the forests became depleted, the town went through an economic depression. A meeting was held to determine what could be done, and it was decided the town should take on a Bavarian theme. Leavenworth became a popular tourist area saving it from bankruptcy.

It was also in Leavenworth that I realized we had a celebrity-look-a-like on the trip. Ever since I met Jeff Bucher (the rider who crashed on the first day), I couldn't figure out who he reminded me of. After some pondering, I finally figured it out: he looked exactly like Bobby Kennedy (the brother of JFK)! I kept asking people in town if Jeff reminded them of anybody, but no one could figure it out. Sadly, most didn't even know who Bobby Kennedy was.

The group stayed at Eastmont High School in Wenatchee, Washington. Despite its rich volcanic soil, the area around Wenatchee was too arid for farming until the Highline Canal was built. Today, Wenatchtee is famous for its apple production. No other region in the world produces more! Even though the land produces a bounty of crops, it was somewhat depressing to look at. The apple trees were green, but the entire land around them was a dingy brown.

<u>Lewis and Clark</u>

Date: June 20, day 3
Start: Wenatchee, WA
End: Moses Lake, WA
Riding time: 4:00
Miles: 70
Maximum speed: 36 mph
Average speed: 17.5 mph
Elevation gain: 2,440 feet
Weather: Sunny and hot, with temperatures in the 80s.

It was a real struggle to finish today.

With the excitement of Stevens Pass behind us, this day's ride was quite a let down.

Traveling along the Columbia River was the only highlight. Lewis and Clark traveled the river and its surrounding gorge in the early 1800s.

Meriwether Lewis and William Clark's expedition was important because it provided scientific information about the animals, plants, and geography of the land. Much of the area has changed little since the two passed through here almost 200 years ago.

The area between Wenatchee and Moses Lake, Washington, has some of the most diverse agriculture in the world. One can see potatoes, sugar beets, cotton, apples, pears, cherries, and corn being grown! The area receives only 15 inches of precipitation per year, so irrigation is very important.

The last 20 miles before Moses Lake were very difficult. It was really hot, and the scenery had suddenly disappeared. I was very glad to finish the day.

Moses Lake is noted for its outstanding sports programs. The high school is home to the three-time defending 4A state wrestling champions, and the town's Babe Ruth baseball team won the Babe Ruth World Series in 1999. For taking home that honor, Moses Lake got to host the 2000 tournament.

Moses Lake was named for the Indian Chief Moses. The closeness of Grand Coulee Dam (60 miles to the north) has raised the water table in the area, creating many lakes and turning it into a tourist area. I know Greg Walsh detoured Coast-to-Coast 2001 and 2002 to include Grand Coulee Dam.

<u>Washtucna</u>

Date: June 21, day 4
Start: Moses Lake, WA
End: Washtucna, WA
Riding time: 4:20
Miles: 72
Maximum speed: 48 mph
Average speed: 16.6 mph
Elevation gain: 2,510 feet
Weather: Sunny and hot, with temperatures near 90.

If you're riding in eastern Washington, be prepared for some rough roads.

The eastern part of the state is very sparsely populated, so the DOT puts little money into roads few people use. Chip seal is often used as a surface. Road construction crews lay down pea gravel and then cover that with tar. It's not only rough, but also dirty. By day's end, my bike and hands were covered with black "gook." It made me appreciate Wisconsin roads.

Wheat is the primary crop grown in the region. It takes two years for a wheat field to get enough moisture to successfully grow a crop. Looking at the fields, there are alternating colors of yellow wheat and brown dirt. The greenish-yellow wheat is ready to be harvested, while the adjacent field sits in fallow, gathering moisture for the following year.

Shortly after our lunch spot, I got my first flat tire. I knew I would get plenty of them, but I didn't figure it would happen so quickly. I had put brand new tires on my bike before the start of the tour. I rode over a set of railroad tracks at too high a speed, and it was enough to blow out my tube. I didn't see them in time to slow down.

When riding over railroad tracks, it's very important to slow down and stay near the side of the road when you go over them. The tracks are less worn near the edges as compared to the middle of the road, so you're less likely to get a flat.

Changing a flat tire is rather simple, but it intimidates a lot of people. I can usually change a flat tire in about five minutes, but sometimes it takes a bit longer. I always carry two tire-irons (devices that help you remove the casing from the rim), a spare tube, and a mini-bike pump with me. After getting a flat, remove the wheel from the bike (most bikes have quick-release levers that allow a wheel to be quickly removed) and then use the tire-irons to remove the casing and take out the old tube. You can either keep the tube and patch it (with a repair kit), or put in a new one. I usually put in a new tube, and then patch the other one at night and use it for a spare. I then take the casing off the rim totally, and check for glass or other debris that may have caused the flat. After checking it over thoroughly, I put one side of the casing back on the rim, and slip in the new tube. It's important to put the new tube in without wrinkling it, because a pinch in the tube can cause it to blow. After the tube is back inside the casing, I put the casing totally back on the rim (using the tire-irons), pump it up, and put the wheel back on the bike.

Our fifth overnight town was Washtucna. Washtucna is one of the oldest communities in Washington.

Washtucna's name translates to "Places of Many Springs." In the early 1800s, Indian groups were able to live there because of the fresh water springs. With only ten inches of precipitation a year (and most of that snow), water is very valuable.

At our nightly meeting, Greg Walsh had invited a community member to speak to our group about the history of the area. The gentleman was a wheat farmer who had lived there his whole life. He thought Washtucna was the absolute best place to live in the whole country.

I've always realized the importance of my small-town up-bringing, but Washtucna reaffirmed that fact. I now realize that there are millions of people across our country who feel the same way about the area they live in, no matter how unfavorably you think of an area. I think it's very important not to judge a book by its cover, and I was guilty of that on this day.

A problem with small towns is keeping the youth around after graduation. The 2000 graduating class in Washtucna had six members. Some kids at the local diner felt there was nothing to stay for.

Washtucna is also having financial problems due to poor wheat crops, so the federal government has stepped in. All children in Washtucna from birth to age 19 are provided a free breakfast and lunch every day. Deep in my heart, I feel it's not only an attempt by the government to help out financially, but a desperate plea to the youth across the country to give back to their local communities.

Many of my fellow riders will question my sanity, but this was one of my favorite days of the summer. It certainly wasn't the most picturesque, but I learned a lot about small-town America. It's a day I think about often.

<u>Floyd</u>

A wonderful part of a cross-country bike tour is the people and their stories.

Bob Goldberg from Seattle is a retired Boeing employee. He had done several shorter tours in his life, but never a cross-country tour. One of his many jobs is organizer for the Seattle-to-Portland (STP) bike ride. During the summer of 1999, Bob was sitting at the registration table for the STP when a woman named Beth approached. She explained how her late husband Floyd, 62, had planned on doing the ride, but died two weeks earlier from his second heart attack in five days. The first attack hit during a 100-mile training ride for the STP. Bob first thought Beth wanted her money back (which is against the STP policy), but soon realized she was there for different reasons.

Beth told Bob that she prayed God would show her a way to fulfill Floyd's dream of riding in the 200-mile event. She had taken one-quarter cup of his ashes and put them in a film canister, put his obituary and a picture of him on it and put it all in a plastic bag. She was looking for someone to carry his ashes. Bob's religious beliefs bar cremation, but he still agreed to carry the ashes.

The ride was anything but ordinary for Goldberg.

The STP attracts up to 7,000 people annually, but there were times when Bob was riding alone...with Floyd. Soon he began talking to Floyd telling him how beautiful the weather and scenery was. The two kept each other company.

Returning home, Bob called Beth and asked if she thought Floyd would like to go on the Ride Seattle to Vancouver Party event (RSVP). Beth agreed.

After completing the RSVP, Bob got another idea: he wanted to take Floyd across the country on Cycle America's Coast-to-Coast 2000 Bicycle Tour. Once again Beth agreed.

On June 18, 2000, in Everett, Beth was there to see her late husband and Bob start across the country.

Bob's story proves that human decency is still alive. He wasn't doing it to gain popularity; he did it from the kindness of his heart.

Over mountain passes, flat land, snow, heat, cold, and headwinds, Floyd would be there with us.

<u>More Lewis and Clark</u>

Date: June 22, day 5
Start: Washtucna, WA
End: Clarkston, WA
Riding time: 5:00
Miles: 90
Maximum speed: 45 mph
Average speed: 18 mph
Elevation gain: 3,860 feet
Weather: Sunny and hot, with temperatures in the 80s.

Did Lewis and Clark have to deal with logging trucks?

When you're riding on a road called the Lewis and Clark Trail, staying in a city named Clarkston and pass through another hailed as Lewiston, you realize the importance of the two men.

Riding on the Lewis and Clark Highway brought about another danger…logging trucks. Traffic was a big concern for me when I signed up for the tour. In northern Wisconsin I'm able to avoid busy streets and head for the scenic back roads. I might go on a three-hour ride and see only a handful of vehicles.

The number of vehicles didn't bother me…it was their high speed. Most were traveling between 70 and 80 mph. Their high speed was due to the openness of the land and the fact that I didn't see any patrol cars.

Cycle America did its best to put us on lesser-traveled roads, but traveling this highway was unavoidable. There simply were no other roads to Clarkston. That's another problem with remote areas. The day was already long enough, and taking a modified route would surely add lots of "bonus" miles.

Even though bicycles are not considered motor vehicles, they have many of the same rights as cars. If this is the case, cyclists must remember to ride responsibly and obey all traffic laws.

I don't think a lot of drivers realize what it's like to ride a bike on a road unless they've done it themselves. Cyclists have a lot to look out for. We have to watch for rocks, glass, tire-wire (the wire from the blown-out tires of semi trucks), nails, bolts, cracks, animals, and other debris.

We also have to bike in less than desirable conditions. On Coast-to-Coast 2000, I rode in pouring rain, through hail on the Fourth of July, endured drastic temperature changes, and dealt with a 25-mph headwind for seven hours. Combine these variables with wanting to see the beauty of the land and it can make for a difficult day. Over the summer I got honked at too many times to count, and in each situation I felt I was being completely safe and responsible.

The worst thing a motorist can do to a cyclist is honk as they pass. It may startle them and cause a crash. Instead, drivers should slow down and leave plenty of room; but if it's not possible due to oncoming traffic, wait until you can safely pass. It could save a life.

The first rule for safe cycling on roads with heavy traffic is to be seen. A tip to cyclists is to "take the lane" if needed. If there is a reasonable distance between you and the traffic behind, slowly pull into the center of the lane. This will force the vehicles behind you to slow to a reasonable speed. This is especially important when crossing bridges, descending hills, riding in town, or riding on roads with no shoulder. It's important that you do this in a safe and responsible manner, though. Remember, if you're not comfortable with this procedure, you can always pull off to the side of the road and wait until the situation is safer. It's also important to wear brightly colored cycling clothes.

Another important tip to cyclists is to **never** make inappropriate gestures or comments to a passing vehicle. It might be enough to cause an altercation!

Also, it's important to use hand signals at the appropriate time when riding a bike on a road. It will give motorists more confidence in you.

About 20 miles after starting, I passed over the Snake River on Washington Highway 261. It was one of the prettiest sights I've ever seen.

I also broke a spoke today. At 150 pounds, I'm a light rider, so broken spokes aren't a problem for me. I guess the rough roads of Washington finally took their toll. It was the first time I had ever gotten a broken spoke, so I not only was surprised, but I didn't know what to do about it, or how to fix it. I had the Cycle America mechanic fix it later that night.

When you get a broken spoke while riding, you should stop right away and remove it or twist it around its neighbors. A flapping rear-wheel spoke can snag the rear derailleur (gear changer) and cause significant damage. I actually descended Alpowa Hill with the broken spoke, as I didn't notice it until near the end of the ride; so I was lucky that I didn't do more damage or crash. Often you can hear it "ping" when it breaks, but I never heard a thing.

Entering Idaho

Date: June 23, day 6
Start: Clarkston, WA
End: Lowell, ID
Riding time: 6:00
Miles: 108
Maximum speed: 33 mph
Average speed: 18 mph
Elevation gain: 2,740 feet
Weather: Sunny and warm, with temperatures in the 70s.

One hundred and eight miles on a bicycle is a long way.

I shouldn't have gone that far, but I took a wrong turn and added a few extra miles. There's really no excuse to get lost on a Cycle America tour because they do such a good job of marking every day's route. As I said earlier, Cycle America hires a route manager to ride the route in a car a day ahead and mark it with yellow arrows. The paint used is DOT approved and wears off within a year. A big joke among the riders was that it wasn't really necessary to attend the nightly meetings because all we had to do was follow the yellow arrows! Needless to say, I still managed to get lost.

Crossing into another state is a big deal, especially on a bike. Some states didn't have border signs, but I managed to get a picture of nine state signs plus Ontario, Canada. I think most of the riders would agree that Wisconsin had the best sign…bar none! It was a huge wooden sign in the shape of the state.

The Idaho landscape is beautiful. It's amazing how the land changes so drastically in only five days of riding. It started with the green forests of the Cascade Mountains and went to the brown sage of eastern Washington. After the sage disappeared, the lush green forests of northern Idaho brought relief once again.

Two cyclists crashed today after being hit by a flag protruding from a passing logging truck. They weren't seriously hurt, but it brought up the issue of safety again. The worst thing about the whole situation was that the truck didn't even stop for our injured cyclists! In all reality, the driver probably didn't even notice he had hit anyone.

Lowell, Idaho, didn't have indoor sleeping arrangements, so I camped for the first time since starting the tour. I didn't have a good tent, so I slept inside whenever I could. I knew it would get old setting it up day after day. I used it ten times the whole trip. If you're planning on attempting such an adventure, I recommend buying a quality tent and a good sleeping pad (things I didn't have).

One of the most commonly asked questions about my cross-country trip is: what did I do when "nature called" and I had to go to the bathroom? I often laugh when people ask me this because it was rather simple. There were so many times during the day that I was away from people, other riders, and vehicles that I simply went when I had to. Knowing that being hydrated is very important, I drank a lot of water, but this caused me to urinate excessively on the trip. I probably stopped an average of six – seven times a day! Defecation is a much bigger problem. Obviously I tried to use restroom facilities when I could, but riding a bike during a bowel movement is impossible; so there were times I had to use "Mother Nature's restroom facilities." Let's put it this way: I left my mark in each state.

<u>Lolo Pass</u>

Date: June 24, day 7
Start: Lowell, ID
End: Lolo Hot Springs, MT
Riding time: 5:00
Miles: 87
Maximum speed: 40 mph
Average speed: 17.4 mph
Elevation gain: 4,640 feet
Weather: Sunny and warm, with temperatures in the 70s.

Another day, another mountain pass.

This was the hardest day so far. It was fitting to end the first segment with a tough day since the next day would be our first day off. This also happened to be the hilliest portion of the trip. I climbed almost 24,000 feet in the first seven days of riding!

Before the trip I invested in an altimeter. An altimeter measures the altitude (height above sea level). It has a small computer chip in it that measures differences in barometric pressure. Barometric pressure changes as altitude does. My altimeter gives me my present altitude, and also keeps track of my elevation gain during a ride.

Although shorter, Lolo Pass was more difficult than Stevens because it came after 72 miles of gradual ascent; by the time I got to the actual climb, my legs were already complaining about their punishment. I wouldn't even had noticed I was going uphill for the first 72 miles hadn't it been for my altimeter.

Lolo Pass is the border between Idaho and Montana, and located on Highway 12. At 5,235 feet it has some historical importance as well. Lewis and Clark passed near here on their journey to the Pacific Ocean. Ancient Indian travel routes from the north, south, east, and west also intersect here. To learn more about the history of the pass, a visitor information center is conveniently located at the top.

It's hard to imagine climbing a mountain on a bike unless you've done it yourself. The Tour de France riders make it look so easy, but it's anything but. For me, climbing a mountain is a love/hate relationship. You forget how hard it is until you do the next one.

Part of the difficulty of the Tour is the mental game. Part of the mental game is putting on a "poker face" when you're struggling. If a rider can see struggle in the eyes and faces of his opponents, an "attack" will likely follow. (An attack is an attempt to break away from your rival riders.) Riders will purposely go to the back of a pack to check things out.

I remember Tour de France winner Lance Armstrong doing this on a climb to Sestrieres, Italy, during the 1999 Tour de France. As he dropped back in the pack, he stared his "victims" in the face to check for signs of weakness. He saw that he was hurting them, so he attacked. He went on to win the stage by 30 seconds and his first Tour de France. Armstrong's opponents were demoralized when they saw no chink in his armor.

Armstrong used his poker face to fool his rivals on a climb to L' Alpe d' Huez during the 2001 Tour. On that day, there were three major climbs, and Armstrong spent the first two at the back of the pack, grimacing with pain. Since all the team cars had TV's, they could see that the fast pace was hurting Armstrong (or so they thought), so they instructed their riders to keep the pace high. When the third and final climb approached, Armstrong slowly moved up, and then attacked. Cycling fans will never forget the "look" he gave Jan Ullrich, a German superstar, as he sprinted away, and took a major step in winning his third Tour de France. Later, Armstrong admitted that he was "faking" the grimacing looks on his face to fool his rivals.

I'm not kidding anyone when I climb…I look terrible. My jersey is wide open, I'm gasping for air, and I'm constantly out of the saddle to keep up my cadence (ideally between 90 and 110).

One of the reasons five-time Tour winner Miguel Indurain seemed so invincible was because his face never showed panic. His hair was perfect, his mouth was always closed, and his jersey was never open. He made it look like he was out on a Sunday morning ride as compared to a stage in the Tour de France. Was he hurting? Of course he was, but he never let other riders know that. In 1996, when he finally lost the Tour, he looked completely different in the mountains. Eventual winner Bjarne Riis of Denmark really made him suffer. Indurain looked vulnerable (not as bad as I do) and Riis could see that.

I love climbing, but the fun comes after cresting the summit. The descent is a cyclist's reward for the hard work getting up the other side.

Besides speed and blown tires, another potential problem on descents is hypothermia. The wind chill can be dangerously low depending on the air temperature. I couldn't believe how cold I got descending, even on warm days.

You'll often see Tour riders put on a wind jacket when crossing a summit. You might even see them grab a newspaper from a fan and stick it in their jersey to act as a wind block.

European cycling is absolutely nuts. The fans are allowed to get very close to the action (sometimes too close). You'll see them running along side their heroes on a climb pouring water over their heads. I've seen instances where a cyclist couldn't even see the road until only a few feet before he got there. It almost looks like the parting of the Red Sea as the crowd spreads out revealing the road. Since I'll never race it, it's my dream to someday see the Tour de France in person and be among the crazed fans.

Most Americans will never fully understand the magnitude and difficulty of the Tour de France, and professional cycling. It's our Super Bowl, but for 23 days. It's like getting your head kicked in every day, for three straight weeks. There are millions of people both on the roadside, and watching on TV. I honestly don't think there is any sporting event equivalent to it.

As one of my training partners says, "Pro Cycling in the U.S. is a lot like church…many attend, but few understand."

To give you an idea of how hard the Tour de France is, I once read an article about how Greg Lemond (the greatest American cyclist before Lance Armstrong) had a diarrhea bout during a stage. As he struggled to the finish, he was surrounded by his teammates. The diarrhea was running down his leg. A "normal" rider would have stopped, but most riders are not capable of winning the Tour. Greg Lemond was capable of winning it (he won it in '86, '89, and '90), and that was the difference in him continuing.

Arriving at camp at 3:00 p.m., I began reflecting on the beauty of the day. I also realized that there were no towns enroute! It gave a new meaning to the word desolate.

One of my fellow riders (who I passed going up Lolo Pass) asked me how I got in such good shape for Coast-to-Coast 2000. I told him that when I trained for the trip, I acted as if I were behind. When he asked me what I was talking about, I told him that if a person wants to improve at something, you need to think that others are better, and the only way to get ahead of them is by putting in hard work. He just smiled at me. I then told him the real reason I was in such good shape…I rode my bike a lot!

He went on to say that I was "flying" up the hill, when in all reality a cyclist doesn't "fly" up a mountain; you crawl, inch by inch, living a slow, agonizing death, and maybe if you're lucky, you make it to the top. A minute can seem like a month when you're pedaling uphill. Like other riders, climbers suffer, but they suffer in a different way. They feel the pain, but they're glad to be there. That's about the only way I can describe it.

Laundry Day

With our first day off came the question of what to do with our laundry. After riding over 500 miles it wasn't something I wanted to worry about, but I knew I had to.

Jeff Bucher helped all the riders spend their first day off worry free…well…almost anyway.

The previous night Jeff walked around camp telling the riders that he had made arrangements for our laundry to be done for only ten dollars. This included washing, drying, and folding. We all thought the deal was too good to be true, but it was certainly better than the alternative…doing it ourselves.

A rotund, elderly woman told Jeff that all interested parties should have their dirty clothes at the motel by 10:00 the next morning. Obviously, the woman didn't know what she was getting herself into. About 25 riders used her service.

Everything seemed to be going okay until we saw the vehicle she was driving. It was an extremely loud and rusted-out Chevy Camaro. We all helped jam the bags of laundry into the car, but could barely shut the door due to its fullness! Soon the lady went roaring off down the highway. We all joked at how stinky that ride must have been for her.

The whole day Jeff was really nervous. He told me that if this deal went sour, he'd be the biggest goat in the state of Montana. No one was more relieved than he when we heard the roar of the Camaro coming down the Lewis and Clark Highway. Everything worked out just fine. No clothes were lost, stolen, or even mixed up. Jeff tried telling everybody he was confident things would work out, but we knew he was lying.

One can't visit Lolo Hot Springs, Montana, without taking a dip in the swimming facilities. There are two separate pools that can literally take your breath away. The indoor one is drained every day and takes eight hours to refill naturally. The temperature ranges from 103-105 degrees, which is hot to the touch. The outdoor facility is a "cool" 90 degrees.

Lewis and Clark passed through here on their journey to the Pacific. They must have liked the springs, because they passed through here again on their return journey.

I also noticed the hot springs in unusual places. It was hard to find a hot shower this summer, but that wasn't a problem here. There was *no* cold water. Also, when I used the toilet, the hot water created steam that rose up out of the privy and made my bottom wet!

When the sun finally set at 10:00 p.m. it got extremely cold. It was the coldest night of the summer and I *had* to camp!

"Mission: Montana"
Montana/Wyoming

The Bitterroots

Date: June 26, day 9
Start: Lolo Hot Springs, MT
End: Darby, MT
Riding time: 4:10
Miles: 83
Maximum speed: 34 mph
Average speed: 19.9 mph
Elevation gain: 1,640 feet
Weather: Twenty-five degrees in the morning, but warming to the mid 80s by day's end.

I don't know why I listened to that store clerk…

About a month before I left Rhinelander for the summer, I went shopping for a sleeping bag. I was looking for a lightweight bag that wouldn't take up a lot of space. Since I didn't think it would get that cold in the middle of the summer, I was persuaded to buy a thin fleece bag. It was actually made to go inside another bag to give added warmth.

As I lay in my tent that cold night in late June, I kept thinking to myself, "Why didn't I bring a better sleeping bag?" I had on long pants, a sweatshirt, gloves, and a hat, and I still almost froze to death! It very well could have been the longest night of my young life.

When I woke up the next morning (I didn't really sleep), there was ice on my tent and the temperature had dropped to 25 degrees! I made a mad dash for the lodge (the bathroom) to warm up.

When it finally warmed up, I rode through the beautiful Bitterroot Valley. The Bitterroot Mountains run along the southwestern border of Idaho and Montana for 200 miles. They are very rugged and have lots of jagged peaks. The highest point in the Bitterroots is Trapper Peak at 10,157 feet.

The first inhabitants of the Bitterroot Valley were the Native Americans of North America.

Death is well documented in the valley, too. Influenza and diphtheria outbreaks were common in the area before antibiotics were discovered. The first white settler cemetery in the Northwest Territory is found here. Native American burial sites have also been discovered in the valley, but the locations are kept secret to prevent vandalism and destruction.

The valley was another stomping ground for Lewis and Clark as well.

Aside from the beauty and historical importance of today's ride, I had my first taste of huckleberries at the "Memories Café" in Corvallis, Montana. Huckleberries are small berries found in the Bitterroot forests. I had them in an ice cream shake, and they were delicious!

Besides being tasty, the word huckleberry gave us a good laugh. All the riders recalled a Clint Eastwood film (Tombstone) where Eastwood can be heard giving one of his famous quotes, "I'll be your huckleberry."

Darby, Montana, was another small town. In small towns you're hard pressed to find any form of entertainment, so you resort to desperate measures. At our evening meal, Jeff Bucher got another crazy idea. Granted, this one wasn't as crazy as the laundry episode, but it would take an equal amount of work.

Jeff noticed a TV/VCR sitting on the table next to our buffet area. He found out who owned it and begged them to let us borrow it for the night. The owners graciously offered the use of the system as long as we returned it the next day. We rented "Notting Hill" starring Julia Roberts. I carried the unit back to the school on my shoulders and we announced our plans to show the movie to the riders. About a dozen people showed up. Although a lot of people did their own "nodding" during the movie, we all had a great time. One of the Cycle America staff members returned the system the next morning.

It was in Darby that I realized I had over-packed. Packing for such a trip is very difficult, but it doesn't have to be. I had to think of all possible weather conditions, so most of my gear was for cycling. My problem came with bringing too many clothes and miscellaneous supplies.

A word to the wise is to only bring what you absolutely need for clothing. Believe me, you won't wear everything you bring. We had access to washing machines whenever we basically wanted, so you can wash as often as you like. If you're doing such a trip, I recommend bringing only one week's worth of clothing for everyday use. You'll thank me in the long run.

As for cycling clothing, you should prepare for all types of weather. You'll need to bring plenty of cycling shorts and jerseys. Good cycling shorts are a must because the chamois (the pad on the inside of your shorts in the crotch area) will reduce chafing and increase comfort. I also recommend a good rain jacket, tights, arm and leg warmers, cycling gloves, a hat and mittens, and booties (socks that go over your shoes to keep your feet warm and dry).

You'll often notice cyclists wearing tight-fitting clothing. Although sometimes it's embarrassing walking around in cycling clothes (because they're rather revealing), it will reduce wind drag while riding. It's estimated that 70 percent of the drag in cycling is caused by the wind resistance of the body. The best way to reduce this is to wear clothing made to fit tighter.

Your cycling gear should include a helmet, a bike pump, spare tubes and tires (although you can buy them along the way), and any miscellaneous bike tools you might need.

My problem came with bringing way too many miscellaneous supplies. When packing, I tried to think of worst-case scenarios, but I should have realized I could have bought any of it during the ride. When I look back, I laugh at all the junk I took (waterless hand cleaner, lotion, cotton swabs, etc.). It was a good bet that if I couldn't find the supplies anywhere, another rider would have been able to help me out. I learned a lot on the trip, especially how to pack for my next one! Believe it or not, I actually started packing for my trip the previous winter (I didn't want to forget anything)!

Instead of lugging two huge bags off the truck every day, I consolidated all my needed gear into one. I put everything that I didn't need into the other bag and put a yellow ribbon on it. I tied a note onto it that read, "Keep on Truck." I had it in my mind to keep it there until I could either ship it home or send it home with my parents if they came to visit.

<u>Hippieville?</u>

Date: June 27, day 10
Start: Darby, MT
End: Jackson, MT
Riding time: 4:50
Miles: 78
Maximum speed: 43 mph
Average speed: 16.3 mph
Elevation gain: 4,500 feet
Weather: Sunny and hot, with temperatures near 80.

The first part of this day's ride included The Lost Trail Pass Climb.

It was a beautiful eight-mile climb at about eight percent. When I envision mountain passes, I think of high winding roads, with sharp drop-offs surrounded by thick green forests. This climb definitely fit that description. (It would all change five weeks later as forest fires ravaged the area, destroying thousands of acres.)

Percent on a climb is figured by calculating how many feet of elevation you gain in 100 feet of travel. For example: if you travel 100 feet and gain ten feet in elevation, the grade is ten percent. If you gain 20 feet in the same distance, it's a 20-percent grade. Anything over six percent is considered steep. Tour riders may climb roads that tilt up to 15 percent.

It took me 40 minutes to do the climb. By the time I reached the top, I had gained 2,200 feet and reached an elevation of 6,995 feet.

Lewis and Clark camped two miles west of the pass on their initial journey to the Pacific.

After lunch, the Chief Joseph Climb came next. It brought me to 7,264 feet and over the Continental Divide. The Continental Divide is a geography term used to describe which way a river flows. If a river is on the western side of the divide, it will eventually flow to the Pacific Ocean. If it's on the eastern side it will end up in the Atlantic.

If you haven't gotten enough history with Lewis and Clark, the area was also made famous by the flight of the Nez Perce Indians.

At mile 47, I was able to relive history as it happened over 120 years ago at the Big Hole Battlefield. It was here that Chief Joseph and his Nez Perce Indians were defeated in a battle by the U.S. Calvary.

History is always easier to learn when you can view it personally. I was able to put myself in the Big Hole Battle of 1877 and relive the moment. I am constantly preaching to my students about the uniqueness of history. History is always happening…every single second.

The only negative that came with visiting Big Hole was the mosquitoes. I've never quite seen them that large.

About ten miles later, I passed through Wisdom, Montana, to get some snacks. The group was supposed to stay in Wisdom, but arrangements couldn't be made. Instead, our destination for the day was the ranching community of Jackson, Montana. Jackson has a population of 45, but in a matter of days, it grew to 30,000 due to the invasion of the "Rainbow Family."

The Rainbow Family is a group of free-spirited individuals, otherwise known as "hippies." They claim their goal is to create a community against violence and hate.

Every year the Rainbow Family plans a yearly gathering somewhere in the United States, and in 2000 they invaded Jackson from July 1–7 for their 28th annual gathering.

The Montana Forest Service requires a permit for any group of 75 or more assembling in the forest. They have these rules because they don't want unnecessary fires or excess trash filling the woods. The problem is that no one from the Rainbow Family was willing to take the responsibility of signing for the permit. Members of the Rainbow Family were told that they would be arrested if they didn't sign.

Another problem is, the Rainbows' sheer numbers will set back the slow-growing pastures of Jackson for years to come. It also had an effect on the local hospital, sheriff's department, and Forest Service.

It's estimated that Beaverhead County's bill topped $175,000 during the gathering. That included unpaid hospital charges, sanitation costs, and stays in the local jail.

I had a chance to talk with the sheriff of Beaverhead County, and he was not only upset with the Rainbows, but with the Forest Service as well.

"Worshipping on public land is fine," he said, "but they're not willing to step forward and be responsible for the negative effects of their actions."

Local residents, whose families have lived here for generations, need a permit to cut a Christmas tree or haul firewood out of the National Forest. They had to watch the Rainbows set up kitchens to feed 30,000, pipe water out of a creek, and dig latrines…permit free!

The Rainbows say they didn't welcome alcohol and violence, but five days **before** the official start of the gathering, there had already been 28 alcohol and drug-related incidents. In addition, 16 felony arrests, 45 misdemeanor arrests, and 6 cases of nudity were reported.

The gathering was quite a shock to the small ranching community.

I, too, could have been a participant of the gathering. When I pulled into camp, a Rainbow member from Tennessee approached me. He invited me to a pre-event celebration eight miles away, but I decided against the idea and spent a quiet night taking refuge from the bird-like mosquitoes.

<u>More Bad Roads</u>

Date: June 28, day 11
Start: Jackson, MT
End: Dillon, MT
Riding time: 2:55
Miles: 49
Maximum speed: 35 mph
Average speed: 16.8 mph
Elevation gain: 2,140 feet
Weather: Sunny and hot, with temperatures in the 80s.

I didn't expect to ride on brand new black top the entire summer, but I didn't anticipate so much gravel, either.

With only 50 miles this should have been an easy day, but the roads made it difficult. You know the roads are bad when you're hoping and praying for chip seal!

Montana is unlike most other states when it comes to road construction. Other states require a project to be entirely funded before it can begin, but the Montana DOT doesn't believe this. Rather than waiting, they feel it's better to begin a renovation and finish it later. When more money becomes available, the project is completed. That's why you'll see so many gravel roads in the state. The vast expanse of land doesn't help, either. Just like Washington, the state isn't going to put money into roads that few people use. Montana is among the top five in land area as well as one of the least-populated states.

Due to the Rainbow gathering a few miles away, the patrol cars were out and about. The police officers also seemed to be a little more ornery than normal.

On two separate occasions, I was stopped by a patrol car and told to get over to the side of the road. He was technically right, but under the circumstances I was a bit perturbed. The closer you ride to the right of the road the more likely you are to get a flat. Nevertheless, I didn't want to get a ticket, so I graciously followed their orders.

A cyclist can often ride in the middle of the lane if no traffic is present, especially out West. It wasn't uncommon to ride for many miles without seeing a vehicle.

It's hard enough to climb and descend a pass on good roads, but on this day I had to "tackle" Big Hole Pass on gravel.

When you're riding on gravel, there are a couple of things you can do to avoid a flat. First off, it's important to have your tires inflated to their maximum tire pressure. Higher tire pressure creates less rolling resistance (where there is actually less rubber from your tire contacting the road). If your pressure is too low when you hit something, the tire will actually form around the object and "engulf" it, allowing it to possibly come into contact with your rim. This in turn can cause a flat. If tire pressure is higher when you ride over debris, objects never get a chance to come into contact with your rim because the high pressure of your tire does not take them in. With less rubber actually riding on the road, there's that much less chance of getting a flat.

It is possible to inflate tires too high, though. If you go too much above the recommended pounds per square inch (PSI), you can blow a tube. I've done this several times in the past, and it's almost as loud as a rifle blast when it blows. Recommended PSI can be found on the casing of your tire.

Recommended PSI varies with different tires. Most road-bike tires vary from 80-130 PSI. The lower the PSI, the more rolling resistance, and in all likelihood, the tire is not built for speed, but for comfort. The higher the PSI, the faster you will go. Although more expensive, higher PSI tires are more durable than lower-pressure ones, because they're often reinforced with Kevlar. I rode 7,000 miles in 2001 with the same front tire, and I didn't get one flat! Good road tires are quite durable, but I think a lot of it is just luck, too.

People who feel my road-bike tires are always amazed at how hard they are. There's more PSI in a good road tire than in a dump-truck tire! To give you some idea, a car tire might have a recommended PSI of 35.

Ninety percent of the time you should have your tires inflated to their maximum tire pressure, but not so when it's raining. In this situation, you want to have more rubber from your tire contacting the road (more rolling resistance) to get a better grip, so decreasing the PSI 15-20 pounds allows this to happen.

One negative with higher PSI tires is a bumpier ride. You will notice *every* bump, but resist decreasing tire pressure too much (unless it's raining) because ***you will*** get more flats. If you find that it's just too bumpy a ride after inflating your tires to their maximum PSI, don't let more than 20 pounds out.

You should check your tire PSI often, because a small amount of air leaks out daily, even with good tires.

If two riders have the exact same fitness, equipment, and weight (your clone), the one with the higher PSI in his tires will go faster with the same effort.

Another tip when riding on gravel is to choose a correct "line." As a cyclist, you never want to cycle with your head down watching the road directly in front of you. Instead, you should focus about 20-30 feet ahead of you to avoid debris and rough road.

Shortly after Big Hole Pass, I passed Beaverhead Rock. Lewis and Clark named the rock, because it looked like a beaver. I didn't really notice it as such when I cycled by it, but upon reviewing my pictures (after completing the trip), I was amazed at the resemblance to the animal.

Another treat was getting caught in a cattle crossing. Although I didn't get to witness it first-hand, other riders estimated that between five and ten thousand animals were in the herd. My timing was bad, so I had to ride through the presents they left behind!

Dillon, Montana, is located on the Beaverhead River in the southwestern part of the state. It was founded with the arrival of the Utah and Northern Railroad. It was named for Sidney Dillon, the president of Union Pacific Railroad. Dillon is primarily a ranching, farming, mining, and tourist area.

<u>Gold!</u>

Date: June 29, day 12
Start: Dillon, MT
End: Ennis, MT
Riding time: 3:55
Miles: 73
Maximum speed: 48 mph
Average speed: 18.6 mph
Elevation gain: 2,730 feet
Weather: Hot and sunny, with temperatures in the 80s.

Gold country!

The Madison Valley lies between the Madison and Gravely Mountain ranges in southwestern Montana.

The valley is primarily cattle country. I saw prize Herefords and Black Angus, along with crops of hay and grain. Timber is harvested from the nearby national forests. Gold mining is also making a comeback in the area, and the valley's talc mine is the second largest in the world.

The Madison Valley is known for its pleasantly cool summer days with temperatures seldom reaching 90 degrees with very low humidity. Wintertime brings snow and cold weather, but the sun shines throughout the season. The valley receives only 12 inches of precipitation a year.

I passed through Nevada City, Montana, at mile 60. Nevada City represents a busy mining town the way it used to be. Two miles up the road, Virginia City is also very historical. It's considered to be the most complete original town of its kind in the United States. It was in Virginia City that I took a break and went for a stagecoach ride. I also visited a few gift shops and actually met someone who knew where Rhinelander was.

When gold was discovered near Virginia City, this brought on "The Rush." Madison County was created in what was then Idaho Territory. Later on, the area was designated the Montana Territory.

Our destination for the night was Ennis, Montana. With the Madison River nearby, Ennis is known as the "Fly Fishing Capital of the World."

Most riders on the trip rode conventional road bikes (with 14-18 gears, and skinny, high-pressure tires), but a few rode very "different" looking ones.

On this night, riders got a chance to "test drive" a different type of bike that was on the trip; it's called a recumbent. A recumbent is a bike on which a rider sits in a "chair-like" seat with their legs straight out in front to pedal, instead of underneath.

Recumbents are very good for people who have back problems, as it takes much of the strain away from that part of the body. It also "saves" your butt from a lot of pain.

The only negatives I found with using the bike were a lack of control and power. Since the controls for the bike are on its side, steering is difficult for many people (including myself). Also, it's very hard to really "stomp" on the pedals to get any sort of power. Using a conventional road bike allows a person to stand up and really put their full effort into each stroke if needed, something you can't do with a recumbent. Therefore, going uphill on a recumbent is extremely slow.

There were several recumbents on the trip, but I used Bob Paiva's (the only other coast-to-coast rider from Wisconsin). Since we had so many riders with a first name of Bob (five total) on the trip, we began giving them nicknames. Bob Paiva became known as "Recumbent Bob."

Earthquake Lake

Date: June 30, day 13
Start: Ennis, MT
End: West Yellowstone, MT
Riding time: 5:20
Miles: 83
Maximum speed: 34 mph
Average speed: 15.7 mph
Elevation gain: 3,730 feet
Weather: Sunny and hot, with temperatures in the 80s.

The bad roads were back.

During the first 14 miles of today's ride, we had seven miles of gravel. Most gravel you can ride on, but this was nearly impossible. The stones were too big and not packed down, so it was difficult to keep my front tire on the ground. (There were times I was only going three mph!) I ended up riding the drainage ditch alongside the road because it was smoother. I also spent some time on the wrong side of the road to find a smoother ride. It was the one day I wish I had a mountain bike. My skinny tires didn't do so well, but miraculously I didn't have a flat.

A mountain bike is a lot heavier than a conventional road bike, but it's equipped with wider tires and a stronger frame, which allow a cyclist to ride over rougher "stuff." If you ride in an area with a lot of debris and gravel (and don't want to worry about many flats), I would recommend a mountain bike as compared to a road bike. Since the tires have knobs on them, though, there is more rolling resistance, so it will be slower. I've owned my mountain bike five years, and I've never gotten a flat.

I was faced with a tough decision about halfway through the gravel. Cycle America was offering van rides to the other end of the construction, but since I wanted to ride *every* mile of the tour, I decided against the idea. I know I would have regretted the "free ride" at the end of the tour.

The roads reminded me of Paris-Roubaix, a 165-mile professional bike race in northern France. Nicknamed the "Hell of the North," it's without a doubt, one of the toughest one-day races in the world. All the professionals want to win it, but none want to ride it. Winners become super heroes. A lot of riders feel they have to ride it to build their reputations, but others feel it's cruel and unusual punishment. You'll seldom see the top stars there.

The race is run for one reason…its bad roads. Thirty miles of the race are run over the worst roads imaginable.

I once heard an interview describing the race:

"On roads made for animals, the enemy is easily recognized. It's not the man who rides alongside you; it's the devil that lurks on the floor. Almost never have more than 40 percent of those who have started reached Roubaix, beaten not by the speed, but by the cobblestones of northern France known as pave'. Man and machinery break under the strain as riders are snatched from their bicycles by forces far greater than theirs. Since 1896, they've all aimed to win the Hell of the North."

There are longer and more difficult races than Paris-Roubaix, but this race is a reminder of the past where riding was pure, and cycling tough. Love it or hate it, every cyclist walks away from the race with stories of luck, good or bad.

It's a constant fight for position, as riders want to be first onto a new section so that they can see the stones clearly. Anyone interested in victory uses a lot of energy to stay near the front.

Run in early April, the weather can be absolutely atrocious. If it's dry, riders can develop conjunctivitis (an inflammation of the membrane lining the inner surface of the eyelid) from the dust, but if it's wet, the pave' turns into a pool of thick slimy mud! The 1994, 2001, and 2002 editions were run in the worst conditions imaginable. They were a cycling photographer's dream, but a rider's nightmare.

The riders' speed over the stones is incredible. Their goal is to get back on smooth pavement as soon as possible, so they push huge gears. Speeds are often in excess of 30 mph.

It's one of the only bike races in the world where the motorcycles that follow the race carry spare tires with them.

There's a big concern among the organizers of the race. Many of the cobbled roads, which date back to Napoleonic times, are being paved over with new asphalt. If the pave' disappears, the race will lose its uniqueness and cease to exist. In an effort to preserve the race, some of the cobbles are being replaced with new ones.

Perhaps Teho de Rooy (a famous cyclist of the past) sums up Paris-Roubaix: "Paris-Roubaix is a pile of shit. You're up to your neck in mud and you're riding and you don't even have time to piss. It's a pile of shit. It's the most wonderful race in the world!"

After lunch I broke another spoke. The gravel didn't give me a flat, but it was responsible for this. It was also extremely windy.

Cycling on, I entered the Madison River Canyon, which was made famous by an earthquake that hit in 1959.

Several faults in the Madison River area moved at the same time causing the earthquake. The resulting slide moved at 100 mph and happened in less than one minute. Over eight million tons of rock crashed into the canyon, burying an open meadow where some campers had stopped for the night. Sadly, 28 people lost their lives.

The landslide completely blocked the Madison River and caused it to form Earthquake Lake, which is 190 feet deep and six miles long. The earthquake measured 7.5 on the Richter scale. Three sections of Montana Highway 287 fell into the lake.

In 1960, a 38,000-acre area in the canyon was designated as the "Madison River Canyon Earthquake Area."

There is a visitor center located on Highway 287, 25 miles to the town of West Yellowstone, Montana, our destination for the day.

Riding through the area, I was amazed at how "present" the earthquake seemed, even after 40 years. It appeared as though it could have happened just yesterday.

This was an extremely hard day for me. Looking back, I don't think I drank enough water. I was too involved in the beauty of the land. That's the only negative about a scenic day; you tend to forget about eating and drinking properly, and focus more on what's around you. Cycle America had given us the option of a shorter route, but if I did that, I'd miss out on most of the scenery.

Although I wasn't in jeopardy of not finishing, the thought of quitting did cross my mind.

Lance Armstrong is a not a quitter. When Lance was 14, his mother got divorced from his step-dad. She was going through a really hard time at work, so Lance told her to quit. His mom snapped back, "Son, you never quit."

This was never more evident than in Armstrong's first professional bike race in 1992, a race called San Sebastian. It's an extremely difficult single-day race in Spain, where riders cover hundreds of miles over demanding terrain, in terrible weather. It was pouring rain and freezing cold, and Armstrong soon found himself at the back of the pack, struggling to finish the day. He faded farther and farther behind, but he kept remembering what his mother had told him. Armstrong knew that he couldn't quit, not in his first pro start. It would be too humiliating. When the day was done, 111 riders managed to finish, and Lance Armstrong was dead last. He finished about 30 minutes behind the winner.

The race changed Armstrong. He not only learned that pro cycling would be a lot harder than he thought, but he gained the respect of his teammates. After the race, he briefly considered giving up the sport entirely. It's a good thing he didn't, because two days later, Lance took second at the Championship of Zurich, and he was destined for greatness. Three years later, Armstrong would get his revenge and become the first American to win a European classic bike race: San Sebastian!

Potato Country

Date: July 1, day 14
Start: West Yellowstone, MT
End: Ashton, ID
Riding time: 2:45
Miles: 50
Maximum speed: 41 mph
Average speed: 18.2 mph
Elevation gain: 1,210 feet
Weather: Sunny and hot, with temperatures in the 80s.

Shortly after starting, I crossed into Idaho.

Our destination was Ashton, the largest seed-potato-producing area in the world. It's also the gateway to the Tetons, a 40-mile-long mountain range along the Idaho and Wyoming border.

At a young nine million years old, the Tetons are known as "The Pilot Knobs" and the "Three Paps." The word Tetons is actually a French word meaning breasts. The highest point in the Tetons is Grand Teton at 13,770 feet.

I developed knee pain on this day. As a general rule, if your knees hurt in front, you should raise your saddle. If the pain is behind the knee, your saddle is too high. Since my pain was behind the knee, I lowered my saddle slightly. You never want to raise or lower your seat too much at one time…a quarter inch is plenty. It gives your knees a chance to adjust to the new height. Sometimes you have to play around with it to get it perfect. Very few people realize that when you move your seat an inch or two, you change the action of every muscle in your lower body, which is involved in the pedaling motion.

Belgian Eddy Merckx was notorious for constantly changing his saddle height, and might even do it during a race!

Nicknamed the "Cannibal" (because he ate up his competition and his appetite for winning was insatiable), Merckx was the finest pro cyclist the world has ever known. He not only won the Tour de France five times, but over 400 other races as well. There were years in the early 1970s when Merckx won over 50 races a year (many pros go a whole career without winning that many). In 1971, Merckx won 54 of the 120 races he entered (45 percent).

Unlike most of today's professionals, Merckx was an all-around rider. He didn't just focus on the major Tours; he raced everything. His season started in February with the European Spring Classics, and didn't end until late October. In 1975, Merckx entered 151 races (winning 38 of them). American Lance Armstrong might have 75 days of racing in one year. In all fairness to Armstrong, though, many of his training rides are as difficult as a race.

For training Merckx used to ride across Belgium (160 miles), take the train home, and then do it all again the next day. He logged over 310,000 miles in his career (it's only 239,000 miles to the moon)! It wouldn't have been uncommon for Merckx to put on 22,000 miles a year.

When asked the formula for success, Merckx responds, "ride lots."

Many of his opponents knew they were racing for second. They felt the only way they could win a race was if Eddy Merckx let them win. If he wanted to win, he simply did it. Merckx made his opponents know they couldn't win. Merckx will be the first to admit that it's hard to compare greatness across sports, but I honestly feel that there's been no other athlete that has dominated his or her sport like he has. This would include Michael Jordan, Tiger Woods, and Wayne Gretsky. Pro cycling is not well known in America, so very few people have heard of him.

All great athletes have a unifying thread, in that they look at not one race, not one game; they look at every race, every game, and every season, and they race to win them all. Like most top athletes in the world, Merckx raced to win them all. Unlike them, he nearly did. He was definitely a perfectionist, but nobody doubted his style because he was so successful.

Eddy Merckx was a person who realized his God-given talents, worked his tail off to develop them into skills, and then used these skills to accomplish his goals. No one has ever been, or ever will be better than Eddy Merckx.

I am definitely not an Eddy Merckx, but like him, I also like to ride alone. I spent the first few days of the trip riding with other people, but I decided that I wanted to start riding alone from here on out. It was nothing against the people I rode with; it's just that I wanted to see the country on my own terms. I wanted to ride at my own speed, stop when I wanted to, and not have to worry about pleasing someone else. I'm so used to riding alone, that it didn't bother me at all.

Arriving in Ashton, we found a TV and tuned in the first stage of the Tour de France. American Lance Armstrong took second place, two seconds behind the winner.

As soon as I finished watching the opening stage, I did some sightseeing in town and did my laundry. I could also see the Tetons, although they were more than 50 miles away. Standing there looking at them, I got somewhat nervous, as I knew the only way to get to Jackson, Wyoming (our next destination), was to go up and over them!

Have you ever gone on a bike trip across several states, and tried to golf in each one of them along the way? It's a hard thing to do, but that's just what Bob Goldberg was trying to do. On short ride days such as this one, Bob would get up early, ride "like the wind," and get to our next destination as quickly as possible. He would shower, grab a bite to eat, and then try to figure out how to get to the local golf course. Most of the time he would bum a ride from Cycle America or find a local resident willing to do the same. Many times, other riders would join him in his quest. Since space was a premium on the Cycle America luggage truck, there was no way Bob could bring his golf clubs from Seattle with him, so he would simply rent clubs at the course. Bob Goldberg became known as "Golfer Bob."

Bob managed to golf in every state except for Washington, but since he lives in Seattle, it was no big deal.

<u>Teton Pass</u>

Date: July 2, day 15
Start: Ashton, ID
End: Jackson, WY
Riding time: 4:05
Miles: 71
Maximum speed: 57 mph
Average speed: 17.4 mph
Elevation gain: 4,430 feet
Weather: Sunny and hot, with temperatures in the 80s.

Today was the tomorrow I worried about yesterday!

I could barely sleep last night because of the excitement of this day. I compared it to a child at Christmas opening presents…my present was Teton Pass!

The first 48 miles were a warm-up for the next 12. Teton Pass is 8,431 feet above sea level. The climb itself starts at the western Wyoming border and goes on for 12 long miles. The bottom portion of the climb is "only" a six-percent grade, but five miles from the top it steepens to 12. I was in my lowest gear and it still wasn't enough. I stood most of the climb. Up to this point, it was the most difficult climb I'd ever done. When climbing, don't think about where you are, but where you want to end up. It will help you make it to the top.

Choosing the correct gearing for a tour or race is crucial. Since none of us were pros, it was better to be over geared.

On Teton Pass I used my lowest gear, a 39 x 25, which wasn't enough. The first number represents the number of teeth on your front chain ring, while the second number is the number of teeth on your back cassette. I recommend three rings in front if you're doing long distance touring (especially if mountains are present). By having two rings in front and seven gears in back, I was able to use 14 different combinations.

I try not to climb in my lowest gear too often (but it was impossible not to on this climb). It's also a good idea to stay seated for as long as possible when climbing, because it uses less energy.

Even though I try, it usually only lasts about 100 yards, then I'm out of the saddle trying to keep my cadence up. I always dread the really steep climbs because I'm my lowest gear right away and I figure, "God…I'm 'screwed'!"

To give you some idea, Lance Armstrong used a 39 x 23-inch gear on many of the mountain climbs in the 2001 Tour de France.

If you're a pro, correct gearing is even more critical. It can be a guessing game, especially on days when there are mountains, flat land, and windy conditions. If you guess wrong, it could cost you a race.

The 1989 World Pro Cycling Championship was won and lost on gearing.

Sean Kelly of Ireland chose a top gear of 53 x 12 for his bike, while American Greg Lemond went with a 53 x 11 (the lower the number in back, the higher the gear). When it came down to the sprint, Kelly "spun" out his top gear as Lemond sprinted to victory. In other words, Kelly's legs couldn't spin any faster in his top gear, while Lemond was still able to put power into each stroke. You wouldn't think that one tooth would make that much difference, but at the pro level, it certainly does. To this day, Kelly feels the mistake in gearing cost him the World Championship, but I'm sure Greg Lemond would beg to differ.

Fifty-seven mph is speeding in most states, so I should have gotten a ticket racing down Teton Pass. If you compare it to American Greg Lemond's 70-mph descent during the 1986 Tour de France, it wasn't that fast!

A bicycle can descend a windy downhill much faster than a car can. On this descent I was catching up to vehicles ahead of me. I got a little worried when I could smell their brakes, but I tried to keep my composure. I felt I was going a little too fast down this descent, so I sat up slightly (to increase wind drag), and pushed my legs against the top tube (the tube that runs from your seat to your handlebars) to gain balance. I'm sure if I had gotten into my "tuck" position (a position of being as aerodynamic as possible), I would have reached 60 mph.

Teton Pass descends into Jackson, Wyoming. When humans started visiting the Jackson area 10,000 years ago, they followed trails across the land that were created by migrating wildlife. Jackson was a crossroads or temporary hunting ground. Winters were too severe for long-term residency. It wasn't until about 150 years ago that year-round residents became a part of the landscape.

With the end of day 15, I took a ride into Jackson for some sight seeing. I bought a $30 steak at a steak house, and milled around town with Bob Patton, otherwise known as "Texas Bob." Jackson is a "tourist town" in every sense of the word. I talked to a lot of people from around the country. Today, Jackson is a winter haven, as there are several ski resorts nearby.

Riding on a bus for eight hours isn't my idea of a day off, but since I had never seen Grand Teton and Yellowstone National Parks before, I eagerly jumped at the chance to tour both of them on our second day off. Greg Walsh set up the tour for us at an additional $40, and it was well worth it.

"Range Ride"
Wyoming

<u>Togwatee Pass</u>

Date: July 4, day 17
Start: Jackson, WY
End: Dubois, WY
Riding time: 5:00
Miles: 94
Maximum speed: 40 mph
Average speed: 18.8 mph
Elevation gain: 4,640 ft
Weather: Sunny in the morning, turning cloudy and rainy, with temperatures in the 50s.

Is it supposed to snow on the Fourth of July?

After a long day touring the national parks yesterday, I was looking forward to a nice quiet ride day. Our ride was "only" supposed to be 65 miles, but it turned out to be 94.

For most of the first 30 miles, I cycled alongside the eastern side of the Tetons; it was very pretty.

At the day's lunch spot, I could see the big challenge of the day off in the distance, Togwatee Pass, an 18-mile climb to 9,558 feet. Even though it was fairly warm and sunny at the base of the climb, I could see the clouds forming above the mountains. I decided to bring along my rain jacket (and I'm glad I did).

About a mile from the top, it began to rain. This was a good example of where my training played a big role in finishing the day. In a matter of 90 minutes, I went from 70 degrees, to 40 degrees and rain!

A word to the wise: always have rain gear with you when you're cycling over a mountain pass. It's very easy to carry extra gear in cycling jersey pockets (which are in the back). The weather can change in a matter of minutes. Togwatee was an example of just such an occasion.

One thing that sticks in my mind from this day is what I saw when I stopped to put on my rain jacket. As I took a few minutes to look around, I glanced behind and was amazed at the tranquility of the

Tetons off in the distance. Even though they were more than 70 miles back, I could still see their beauty. It looked like a painting.

The climb wasn't really steep, but it was extremely cold. For some reason, I felt like a mountain goat on the climb. It probably had something to do with the fact I spent the previous day riding in a bus for eight hours.

Ironically, the term mountain goat is synonymous with the non-climbers (sprinters) in the Tour de France. You'd think it would be the opposite, as mountain goats are just about the best climbers around, but not in cycling terms.

The sprinters have their glory during the flat stages, but once the mountains start, they struggle to finish each day. You'll seldom see them still in the race after the mountains because they can't get their big bodies over the passes like a small climber can. The climbers have thin legs and weigh very little, while the sprinters have huge legs and weigh a lot more.

Many of the best climbers in the world weigh only 130 pounds, while the sprinters can weigh up to 200 pounds. Seventy pounds on a climb is an astronomical difference. On a mountainous day, it's not uncommon for the sprinters to finish 30 minutes behind the winner. Anyone interested in final victory has to be able to climb, so you'll never see a sprinter winning a mountainous race (except Eddy Merckx).

One of the neatest things to see is a climber getting ready to attack on a climb. An attack on flat land can be neutralized by just about anyone, but when a climber goes, there's little the non-climbers can do.

I'm not positive what makes a good climber, but genetics, lightness, attitude, and training have a lot to do with it; although, it's not one single factor that makes the difference.

The top of Togwatee had an eerie calm to it. I was all alone, 9,600 feet above sea level, with a light drizzle falling, and the temperature was only 40 degrees! I took a few minutes to enjoy the peace and quiet, and also took the opportunity to make a snowball. I had to jump a fence to do it, but I figured it would be the only spot on the trip where I would be able to make one (and it was).

On the way down I got caught in a thunderstorm and almost froze to death. It was really touch-and-go for a few minutes, as the roads were really slick. Looking back, I should have gone a lot slower, but in only 15 minutes, the rain stopped and the sun came out (another example of a drastic temperature change).

During long descents on wet roads, it's ***extremely*** important to maintain slight brake-pad contact with the rims to keep them free of excess water and allow for quicker stopping. Make sure you don't put too much pressure on them, though, or your rims may heat up too much, causing a tube to blow.

If I hadn't had my rain jacket, I'm sure I would have developed hypothermia. I covered the last 30 miles from the summit to camp in 70 minutes.

If I had to climb another pass today, it would have been nearly impossible, because my legs could barely get me up the only climb of the day. I worked up a huge sweat ascending Togwatee, but on the way down my muscles really tightened up because I wasn't pedaling as much.

Many times on a mountainous day, pro riders have to climb more than one pass, so that's why it's so important for them to keep warm on the descent. Unlike the recreational cyclist who coasts downhill, pros often pedal as fast as they can to gain time and keep warm.

When descending, you'll find your bike will be more stable if you are pedaling, not just coasting. Always descend in high gear to retain the ability to accelerate if the situation calls for it.

I would spend my Fourth of July in Dubois, Wyoming. It's named after Senator Dubois from Idaho.

It's not uncommon to have snow in mid-June in Dubois. I was told that it had snowed on the Fourth of July several times in the past.

Thirty miles southeast of Dubois lay Crowheart Butte. A butte is a flat-topped hill with steep sides. The area was a battleground among the Indians who were fighting for hunting rights.

It was in Dubois where I learned how hard a cross-country bike tour is mentally. Physically, the miles were ticking away beneath my tires, but mentally I was caving in. Even though I was having a blast, I was lonely and questioning my sanity.

I made the mistake of calling home when I got done with my ride. I called home every day to give an update, but I should have known better on this day. I guess I was feeling a bit lonely. When my sister picked up at the other end, it sounded like there were a 100 people at my parents' house. They were having a great time celebrating the Fourth of July, while I was in the middle of Wyoming freezing to death. If I could have gone home for that one day (and then come back) I would have. I hung up as quickly as I could and went and watched the parade downtown.

<u>Red-Rock Formations</u>

Date: July 5, day 18
Start: Dubois, WY
End: Riverton, WY
Riding time: 3:50
Miles: 78
Maximum speed: 37 mph
Average speed: 20.4 mph
Elevation gain: 1,510 feet
Weather: Sunny and hot, with temperatures in the mid 90s.

Cyclists love tailwinds, and on this day there was a great one!

I covered the first 40 miles at a 22-mph clip. I've learned to take advantage of a good wind, as it can change at the drop of a hat.

I also saw some beautiful red-rock formations. Some of the rock is estimated to be over 600 million years old! Since I was in dinosaur country, I wondered to myself how many fossils of the giant beasts were covered in that rock.

I was also surprised at the openness of the land. Growing up in the U.P. of Michigan, I thought I knew what desolate was, but the West gives a whole new meaning to the word. It was common not to see another vehicle, person, or town for many miles. I am definitely a small-town person, but it takes a special type of person to live in areas like this. In Idaho and Montana it too was desolate, but the land was covered with trees. Wyoming doesn't have much of anything on the land.

The weather was also extremely hot. When the temperature rises, it's very important to keep yourself hydrated. Dehydration is the number-one reason for fatigue. As a general rule of thumb, a cyclist should drink every 15 minutes while riding, but more when the temperature rises. You should drink before you're thirsty, and eat before you're hungry. You want to drink enough to keep hydrated, but not so much that urination becomes a problem. In hot weather, two bottles of water should be drunk for every hour of cycling.

Your body is made up of 60 percent water, so that's why it's so important to keep hydrated. Studies show that a deficit of just four percent can decrease your body's performance by 50 percent!

Even though hot, the West is very dry, so a person doesn't sweat for very long. With humidity near ten percent, I wasn't uncomfortable, even if the temperature was close to 100 degrees.

Arriving in Riverton, Wyoming, I talked to a life-long resident at the high school and got a good feel for the area.

He told me that the biggest export in Wyoming is the kids. They go to college in Wyoming, and then when they graduate, there are no engineering or other professional jobs for them here, so they leave in search of work. Just as I said about Washtucna, if the youth leave an area it will cease to exist. It's a community's job to make sure they do everything possible to keep youth around. The area around Riverton is famous for its deposits of uranium, oil, and natural gas. It's also home to the Riverton Wolverines. The boys' football team won the 3A football state championship from 1997 – 1999.

When I think of Wyoming winters, the word harsh comes to mind. Granted, many parts of Wyoming get lots of snow and cold temperatures, but Riverton is not one of them. Riverton gets only 12 inches of precipitation a year. Seeing that the city doesn't even own a snowplow, I guess the winters aren't too bad!

Riverton is named such because of its location near the convergence of four Wyoming rivers (Beaver, Bighorn, Sweetwater, and Wind).

Another must-see attraction about 40 miles west of Riverton is the grave of Sacajawea. Sacajawea was an Indian guide that traveled with Lewis and Clark on their journey to the Pacific.

In what was becoming a nightly ritual, Bob Haley from New Jersey, put all the riders to sleep with a beautiful trumpet rendition of "Taps." Taps is a bugle or trumpet call sounded at night at military camps as an order to put out lights. In the morning, Bob would play "Reveille," the twin to Taps, but only played in the morning as a wake-up call. Bob Haley became known as "Trumpet Bob."

<u>Dinosaur Country!</u>

Date: July 6, day 19
Start: Riverton, WY
End: Worland, WY
Riding time: 4:30
Miles: 92
Maximum speed: 43 mph
Average speed: 20.4 mph
Elevation gain: 2,020 feet
Weather: Sunny and hot, with temperatures in the mid 90s.

I wonder who invented tire-wire?

This day was very scenic, as it was definitely one of the prettiest days of the whole trip. For starters, there were plenty of red-rock formations for us to view and the Wind River Canyon to ride through.

Flat tires were a problem for a lot of riders, though. I didn't talk to too many of them who didn't experience one. One rider got five! She got some tire-wire wrapped through her tire, and it caused a lot of havoc. Tire-wire is very small, thin, and hard to see. It can get wrapped up in your tire and you might not even notice it. It's important to thoroughly check your casing after a flat because if the wire is still in there, you'll get another one. This obviously happened to her. Be careful not to cut yourself while doing so, though. I ended up getting a flat tire as well.

What kind of water would be in the Badwater River? Right before entering the Wind River Canyon, I cycled over it. As I peered down to take a look, the river was completely dry! I thought to myself, "Now that's some bad water."

A highlight of the canyon was the tunnels I rode through. Although they weren't more than a hundred yards long, they were completely dark.

After riding through the canyon, I came upon Thermopolis, Wyoming. Thermopolis is home to the world's largest hot spring. Almost four million gallons of hot spring water is produced here a day! If you're ever in the area, make sure you stop and take a dip.

The area is also very famous for its dinosaur collections. Many of the best dinosaur specimens in the world have been discovered in Wyoming.

Worland, Wyoming, is a tourist area for people traveling to Yellowstone. It used to have a big oil business, but that has since passed. The rodeo is what helps the community thrive now.

The southwestern part of Wyoming was suffering from wildfires, too. When I looked to that part of the sky, I could see a gray haze in the air. The Rock Springs fire had already consumed 22,000 acres, and was considered zero percent contained at this point. With winds approaching 20 mph and temperatures in the 90s, the outlook was bleak.

Big Horn Mountains

Date: July 7, day 20
Start: Worland, WY
End: Buffalo, WY
Riding time: 5:40
Miles: 93
Maximum speed: 55 mph
Average speed: 16.4 mph
Elevation gain: 8,400 feet
Weather: Sunny and hot, with temperatures in the mid 90s.

Vince Lombardi once said, "Fatigue makes cowards of us all."

Two days ago, one of my fellow riders asked me why I put in over 8,000 training miles in the last year to prepare for this trip, when I could have put in a lot less? I now know the reason…July 7, 2000. This was a day that I wanted to prove something to myself, and when a person has something to prove, there's nothing greater than a challenge.

When I signed up for the trip in 1999, I wasn't going to cheat myself when it came to training. As I mentioned earlier, it's possible to do a cross-country trip with far less miles in your legs, but the more you put in, the more you'll be able to enjoy yourself.

This ride was an absolute brute. It took us over the Bighorn Mountains (named for the incredible number of Big Horn Sheep in the area) in north central Wyoming. Up until this point, I've never had a tougher ride on my bike, but also none more rewarding. This was a day that tested my strength and endurance, both physically and mentally.

The actual climb over the Bighorns begins at mile 27 (from Worland) in Ten Sleep, Wyoming, with an elevation of 4,200 feet. Ten Sleep is a small mountain village nestled in the foothills near the Big Horn Mountains. If you're ever near Ten Sleep, you'll want to take in Bates Battlesite, an engagement in which the Arapahoe Indians were defeated by a coalition composed of U.S. troops and the

Shoshones. The battle gave the white man control of the Big Horn Mountains.

The Powder River Pass Climb (the climb over the Bighorns) was a full 30 miles! At six percent, the grade wasn't too severe, but the shear length of the climb had its effect on my body. At mile 44 and an elevation of 7,800 feet, I stopped for lunch. I didn't stay long as I wanted to continue to the top. I still had another 12 miles and 1,800 feet to climb.

Reaching the top at an elevation of 9,666 feet (our highest point of the trip), I was ecstatic. Mentally and physically there is such relief when you reach the top of a pass.

Powder River Pass is a lot different than any other mountain pass I've ever climbed. It is really dry (at least on this day) compared to the others.

Joe Stun from New Jersey had a funny experience while climbing Powder River Pass.

"Jersey Joe" is a big guy at over 200 pounds, and he'll admit that he struggles somewhat on the climbs, but he enjoys them, too. A couple from Oklahoma pulled up alongside him in an RV and told Joe that they were having trouble breathing at the high elevation. They wanted to know if Joe was having trouble as well. Keep in mind, that Joe was *riding* his bike up a 30-mile climb, and the couple was *driving* in an RV!

A person who lives at sea level may have a difficult time going to a higher altitude due to the lesser amount of oxygen. A person who lives at higher elevations has more red blood cells, which carry oxygen. The longer you stay at higher elevations, the easier it becomes to breathe, because your body begins to manufacture more red blood cells. Many athletes get a natural high by training at altitude and then coming down to sea level. They create more oxygen-carrying red blood cells for their event. The effects may last for weeks or even a month, but gradually at a lower elevation the number of red blood cells will decrease in your body. You can bet that Lance Armstrong does a lot of training in the mountains prior to the Tour de France to get his body ready.

If you're planning on vacationing in an area with a higher elevation, you need to be careful about Acute Mountain Sickness.

You may experience flu-like symptoms for a few days until you get used to the change. It's important that if you're doing any physical activity, you wait a few days to let your body adjust. The longer you wait, the more adapted your body becomes.

Did you know that if a person were flown to the top of Mount Everest, they would be unconscious in two minutes and dead within five? Climbing Mount Everest is a ten-week process. The climbers spend weeks letting their bodies adjust to the different elevations.

It's important that a person drink more water at high elevations, too, because dehydration occurs more rapidly. Sunburn and the effects of alcohol and other drugs are dramatically increased as well. A person drinking at 6,000 feet will get drunk twice as fast as a person at sea level.

Finally, nosebleeds can occur with high elevations. Our oldest rider at 71 got them.

Although I can't say for sure, I don't think I had any problems with the higher elevation. When I was climbing, I could never figure out if I was breathing hard due to the thinness of the air, or the fact that I was going up hill.

After I got my picture taken at the top, I started my descent.

At the previous night's meeting, we were told that once we hit the top at mile 57, there were 35 miles of downhill to enjoy. The so-called 35-mile downhill was not meant to be. The first few miles were steeply downhill (I hit 55 mph), but it quickly changed. On the third or fourth mile-long climb **after** the top, I realized the information from the meeting was not accurate. I didn't get upset about it; I took it as a challenge. I love to climb, so I was happy. The more enthusiasm you have for something, the more successful you'll be. I wasn't going to get angry, because I knew it would affect my performance. Miles 57-85 were like a roller coaster. I think those 28 miles were actually tougher than the climb itself.

It wasn't until mile 85 that the actual descent into Buffalo, Wyoming, took place. Buffalo's elevation is 4,600 feet, so it's true that we did go downhill from Powder River Pass, just not in the typical fashion.

Some descents are not made for bicycles and this was one of them. In many Western states, cattle crossing the roads can be a big problem. To combat this, cattle grates are placed in the middle of the road. They are metal grates that prevent the cattle from crossing. Underneath the grate, the road is hollowed out. Most of the time the cattle are afraid of them and they won't attempt to cross because they'll fall through and get stuck. Going over these at 40 mph is extremely dangerous, but it's hard to spot them ahead of time. Since I was the first to descend that day, I had no way of knowing they were there. Later on, riders positioned themselves up the road to warn other cyclists. The DOT even paints fake cattle grates on the roads. Apparently cattle aren't too smart!

Ted Roehrig from Pennsylvania had his own "meeting" with the cattle grates.

Ted claims that his morning dose of orange juice took its usual affect about an hour after leaving breakfast. Since he was out in the middle of nowhere, he leaned his bike up against a fence post and began concentrating on the job at hand. There happened to be a cattle grate nearby, but he made sure that he stood perpendicular to it so he wouldn't fall through. I guess his short-term memory failed him, because when he turned to go about his business, he forgot about the grate and fell through! Thankfully, Ted stopped about six inches from his groin. Ironically, Ted was more worried about people seeing him (no one did) than the physical pain he was enduring.

He managed to pull himself out of the mess, and then realized that he was probably dumber than the cattle because they knew enough not to fall through.

A lot of people were not happy at that night's meeting. They felt they were basically lied to at the previous night's meeting. Personally, I think most people relied on the informational meetings too much. I think a lot of cyclists learned a valuable lesson on this day…don't take training for granted.

With 8,400 feet of elevation gain, this day's ride ended up being the hilliest of the whole summer. If you compare it to a tough Tour stage, when the riders climb 20,000 feet and six passes in one day, it wasn't too bad!

Perhaps a rider summed up the day at dinner by saying, "Isn't there an easier way to commit suicide?"

<u>Coal Country</u>

Date: July 8, day 21
Start: Buffalo, WY
End: Gillette, WY
Riding time: 4:20
Miles: 75
Maximum speed: 35 mph
Average speed: 17.3 mph
Elevation gain: 3,470 feet
Weather: Sunny and hot, with temperatures near 90.

Riding a bicycle on an Interstate sure isn't very much fun.

If I was to ride my bike on the Interstate in Wisconsin, I could, and probably would get a ticket, because it's illegal. But in Wyoming (and several other states out West) it's perfectly *legal* to do. In many cases Interstate roads are the only way for bicycles to get from town to town, because there are no other roads. Even though there were other roads that could have gotten us to our destination, on this day, we took the Interstate to avoid added miles.

After a rather difficult day yesterday, everybody was ready for an easy day. Unfortunately, Mother Nature has a strange way of dealing with tired bike riders.

The first 35 miles were fast due to a nice tailwind, but suddenly the tailwind turned into a nasty headwind, and the last 40 miles were very difficult.

Riding on an Interstate can be very challenging, but mainly it's very boring. If you took a poll of the riders, many would tell you that today was the most boring of the summer. There simply wasn't much to see or do. It was a matter of just getting done.

Interstate traffic can be tricky, too. On most Interstates, there is a ridge of bumps on the shoulder to prevent people from going into the ditch. The idea is that if a person falls asleep at the wheel and begins to drift off the road, the ridges will shake the car and wake them up. The dilemma is deciding what side of the ridges to ride on. If you ride on the left side, you are closer to traffic, but there is less debris.

If you ride to the right of the ridges, you are further away from the cars, but also in the middle of a lot of junk.

Another tricky situation with Interstate riding comes with the exits. A bike has to quickly race across the exit ramp to get to the other side. A car that is speeding to an exit doesn't want to have to slow down, so you have to be sure the coast is clear.

Gillette, Wyoming, located in Campbell County, is one of the fastest growing cities in Wyoming. If Campbell County were its own country (it would be small), it would be the world's fourth leading producer of coal!

Gillette is also the former home of a professional football player named Ryan Christopherson. He went to college in Wyoming before being drafted by the Jacksonville Jaguars in the fifth round of the 1995 draft. He went to college in Wyoming after graduation and then got drafted. Although I'm not sure if he's still playing, it was neat to be in the same hallways where a pro football player once roamed.

The night before the last ride of the week is traditionally awards night. Awards are given to other members of the group to remember a moment during the week. Up to this point, I hadn't received or given one, but I changed that tonight.

A few days ago, Jersey Joe had been complaining to me about his sore butt. He told me that if he only had a banana peel, he could slip it in his shorts and that would do the trick. I thought that if I could find one, I would give it to Joe as a gift. Rummaging through the garbage can, I found what I was looking for and presented it to him. I know he appreciated it, but I'm not sure he used it!

Due to other commitments and jobs, a lot of people could only bike for a week or two of the summer. Only 52 of us did all nine segments and went coast-to-coast. Awards night was always an emotional time of the week because we knew many of the riders would be leaving the next day.

<u>Devils Tower</u>

Date: July 9, day 22
Start: Gillette, WY
End: Devils Tower, WY
Riding time: 3:40
Miles: 71
Maximum speed: 44 mph
Average speed: 19.3 mph
Elevation gain: 2,060 feet
Weather: Cloudy, with temperatures in the 70s.

There were certain days during the summer when your destination was your main focus. This day was just like that.

I wanted to get done at a reasonable time so I could view Devils Tower. In 1906, President Roosevelt proclaimed it the first national monument in the United States. By doing so, Wyoming was home to both our first national park (Yellowstone) and our first national monument.

Devils Tower is a giant rock-like structure that juts up into the sky 867 feet. Scientifically, it's a failed volcano that didn't have enough force and pressure to breach the surface of the earth. It wasn't until millions of years after its creation, when the surrounding land eroded away, that the rock was exposed. The area of its top is one-and-one-half acres and its diameter is 1,000 feet.

If you don't believe the scientific reasoning behind its existence, maybe you'll enjoy the Native American version. This one seems to be the most popular:

"One day, an Indian tribe was camped beside the river and seven small girls were playing at a distance. The region had a large black bear population and a bear began to chase the girls. They ran back toward their village, but the bear was about to catch them. The girls jumped upon a rock about three feet high and began to pray to the rock, 'Rock take pity on us; Rock, save us.' The rock heard the pleas of the young girls and began to elongate itself upwards, pushing them higher and higher out of reach of the bear. The bear clawed and jumped at the sides of the rock, and broke its claws and fell to the ground. The bear continued to jump at the rock until the girls were pushed up into the sky, where they are to this day in a group of seven little stars…the Big Dipper."

The "marks" of the bear claws are there yet. As one looks upon the tower and contemplates its uniqueness, it isn't hard to imagine this legend as fact.

Not only is Devils Tower a beautiful site, but it's also a paradise for climbers.

Since 1937, approximately 50,000 climbers have made their way to the top. Five thousand climbers come here every year from all over the world. Due to climbing inexperience, two climbers have died in the last five years.

Our massage therapist almost found this out the hard way. He was making an attempt at climbing the tower on our day off. Climbing with no equipment, he didn't get very far. About 250 feet up, he got himself into an awkward position and had to back down. Talking to him afterwards, he was just relieved to make it down in one piece.

About a year later, I discussed his attempt with a friend who has climbed the tower several times, and he couldn't believe a person would attempt such a thing with no equipment. My friend was actually surprised that he didn't end up killing himself.

On my third day off, a few of us "bummed" a ride from a passing vehicle to the base of the tower, and then we were able to make the mile-and-a-half trek around it. You can't imagine how big it is until you see it up close.

There's more to the area than the tower.

More than 150 species of birds, white tail deer, and prairie dogs can be found in and around the area surrounding the tower.

The area was also made famous by the movie "Close Encounters of the Third Kind." After the movie was released in 1978, visits to the tower jumped dramatically. The KOA campground near the base of the tower shows the movie every night in an outdoor facility. I attempted to watch it, but I quickly dozed off.

Sid Clark from Colorado acquired quite a reputation as being a very loud sleeper. I would put him up against anyone! It started way back in Skykomish (our first overnight) when I had to leave the gym that night to get away from it all. I've never heard a person snore louder in my life. If the trains weren't going, you could count on Sid. He had a great sense of humor, though, so he would put orange cones around the perimeter of his tent to warn the new riders. It soon became a game of cat and mouse. I made sure that if Sid was outside, I was inside, and vice versa. It was really funny when new riders would join us for the week and they would inquire about the orange cones. At Devils Tower, there was no one within a 30-foot radius of his tent!

"Monumental Memories"
Wyoming/South Dakota

<u>July 4th Fireworks</u>

Date: July 11, day 24
Start: Devils Tower, WY
End: Newcastle, WY
Riding time: 4:00
Miles: 77
Maximum speed: 44 mph
Average speed: 19.3 mph
Elevation gain: 4,360 feet
Weather: Partly cloudy and hot, with temperatures in the 80s.

The Fourth of July…a week late!

Since I didn't get to see fireworks on the Fourth of July, a few local juveniles took care of that for me. Unfortunately, it happened in the middle of the night!

Newcastle, Wyoming, wasn't one of my favorite overnights on the trip. It's a railroad town, so every 30 minutes throughout the night I heard a train pass by. I would just start to doze off and the next locomotive would come barreling through. To combat this, I tried sleeping inside the school's gymnasium, but that didn't work because of the unbearable heat, so I moved outside on the sidewalk. Since it was in the middle of the night, I didn't even bother setting up my tent. I just moved my foam pad out on the sidewalk and tried falling asleep. That's when the fireworks started…literally.

I awakened to the sounds of bottle rockets and fireworks, some only a few feet away from me. I thought it was all a bad dream, until many of the riders complained about the same thing the next morning. Since the next day's ride would be short and beautiful, I didn't dwell on it too much, though.

Newcastle was named after a town of the same name in England.

Earlier in the day I got a taste of the Black Hills. Most people think that the Black Hills are entirely in South Dakota, but that's not true. Good portions of them are in Wyoming, too.

In what was becoming a nightly ritual, we *had* to find a TV. The Tour de France had started a few days earlier and we had to check up on Lance Armstrong's progress. On this day, he took over the Yellow Jersey by over four minutes. I told the other riders that as long as Armstrong didn't crash or get sick, the Tour was his. My prediction came true a couple of weeks later.

You might be wondering what the Yellow Jersey is? Each day at the Tour, four different colored jerseys are awarded.

The Yellow Jersey goes to the rider that is leading the race overall on time. Since Armstrong was over four minutes up on his next rival, he had actually spent four less minutes riding so far. The Green Jersey is given to the most consistent finisher in the peleton (the French word for a group). It takes a special rider to wear this jersey, because he not only has to be a good sprinter, but a good climber as well. The third jersey is the Polka Dot Jersey. It's given to the best climber in the race. Riders gain points as they reach the summit of mountain passes. The more difficult the climb, the more points they gain. The last jersey is the White Jersey. This is given to the best young rider under 25 years of age.

Since Eddy Merckx could sprint and climb, he's the only rider to ever win all three jerseys in the same Tour, doing so in 1969 (they didn't have the White Jersey back then).

Speaking of TV, I didn't get to watch it often. Since a lot of TV is fantasy, and I was smack dab in the middle of reality, I didn't mind not watching it. The only TV that I really watched was the Tour. There simply was no access to it at any given time.

A Day in Paradise

Date: July 12, day 25
Start: Newcastle, WY
End: Custer, SD
Riding time: 3:00
Miles: 52
Maximum speed: 45 mph
Average speed: 17.3 mph
Elevation gain: 3,640 feet
Weather: Sunny and hot, with temperatures near 90.

Today was a touring cyclists' dream.

The weather was perfect, the scenery was beautiful, and the mileage was short. Add it all up, and you have a day in paradise.

After only 12 miles, I entered the Black Hills of South Dakota. The name came from the early explorers who said the land had so many pine trees that it appeared to be black. The Black Hills cover 6,000 square miles. The region is one of the richest gold-mining districts in the United States and contains a wide variety of other natural resources.

A few miles after entering South Dakota (my fifth state), I stopped at Jewel Cave. Jewel Cave is the second longest cave in the world. The only one larger is Mammoth Cave in Kentucky. Mammoth has 20 natural openings compared to Jewel's one.

After no valuable resources were found in the cave, it was turned into a tourist attraction. Although it was never a tourist success, Jewel Cave was established as a national monument.

In a matter of minutes, I was 400 feet below the surface of the Earth via elevator. Entering the cave, I found the humidity to be extremely high. It stays between 88 and 92 percent year round. At 49 degrees, the temperature also remains constant all year. It may vary one-half degree from summer to winter. Jewel Cave was one of the highlights of the trip for me.

Outside the cave I was able to visit with some Wisconsin natives. No matter where I was in the country, I could always find someone who lived close to my home. Maybe they were attracted to my ugly farmer's tan (I had my shirt off), which I had acquired after three weeks of riding.

The Crazy Horse Monument was my next destination, but first I had to descend "Hell's Canyon," a narrow, curvy, road that tested my bike-handling skills. Our route manager had told us this was a *very* dangerous descent, but I didn't think it was bad at all.

Crazy Horse was a Sioux Indian leader born near Rapid Creek, South Dakota. To the Sioux, Crazy Horse was a patriot and battle hero. He became popular among other Indian groups because of his resistance to the U.S. occupation of Indian country.

Once completed, the Crazy Horse Monument will be the largest mountain carving in the world (563 x 641 feet). Since it's privately funded (no money from the federal government), it's impossible to say how much longer it will take to complete the carving. It could take another 50 years.

I can't believe how mammoth the carving is. After locking my bike up at the visitor's center, I rode a shuttle bus to it, and that really put its size into perspective.

If you visit the monument, you will notice Crazy Horse's arm outstretched pointing towards the Black Hills of South Dakota. When an officer asked him, "So, where are your lands now, Crazy Horse?" The Indian pointed to the horizon and responded, "My lands are where my dead lie buried."

The statue is not only a tribute to Crazy Horse, but also to all Native Americans.

The group stayed at the Flintstone Campground in Custer, South Dakota. Custer is the oldest town in the Black Hills. It's named for Lt. Colonel George Armstrong Custer.

Historians say it was Custer's journey into the Black Hills that touched off the gold rush and led to his humiliation near the Little Big Horn River two years later. Ironically, the leader of the Sioux Indians against Custer in that battle was Crazy Horse.

Custer is also home to Custer State Park, a 73,000-acre reserve, and home to the largest free-roaming bison herd in America.

I often tell people that Custer was my favorite town on the trip. With the Black Hills all around, it's very beautiful.

<u>Mount Rushmore</u>

Date: July 13, day 26
Start: Custer, SD
End: Rapid City, SD
Riding time: 4:45
Miles: 83
Maximum speed: 46 mph
Average speed: 17.5 mph
Elevation gain: 6,500 feet
Weather: Sunny and hot, with temperatures close to 100.

Even though physically this was a very hard day, I hardly even noticed. My mind was too preoccupied with the beauty around me to notice anything else.

Cycle America had given us the option of several different routes. I could have gotten to Rapid City, South Dakota, in as little as 50 miles, but I knew if I did that, I'd miss out on the best part of the ride. Some riders had been opting for the shorter routes for quite some time now. They were getting tired and wanted to take the shortest route between the starting city and our ending destination. Some of them even made up their own routes to get to the next town. In contrast, I often added miles to take in additional sites.

Right out of Custer I began an eight-mile 1,200-foot climb. The road, "Needles Highway," reminded me of Wisconsin, except it was a lot steeper. "Needles" is perhaps the most scenic highway in America. Certainly I haven't ridden on a prettier road. It's a windy, narrow back road that takes you through the heart of the Black Hills. You will ride through tunnels, see buffalo and mountain goats, and be able to view Mount Rushmore.

Needles also gave me my first look at steaming hot buffalo dung. I actually stopped and took a picture of it, as I thought I might use it as a bathroom pass for my class!

Right after seeing the buffalo dung, I had to stop because there was a pack of wild burros blocking the road. There were about six cars stopped as well, so after putting my arm around one of the donkeys, I asked a motorist to take my picture.

I also got to visit Mount Rushmore, named for New York lawyer Charles E. Rushmore. The worst thing about viewing it was the two-mile, ten-percent climb to get there!

It took 14 years to complete all four heads. Only six-and-one-half years were spent on the actual carving, as money was the main problem during the Great Depression years.

Many of the riders thought the Crazy Horse Monument was more spectacular, but I was partial to Mount Rushmore. Although not as massive, I was awed by its presence. Crazy Horse's surface appeared to be rough and dirty, but Mount Rushmore was smooth and clean. Maybe it was because I couldn't get as close to Rushmore and see it as well, but I figure the real reason is that the federal government funds its upkeep. The only negative of Mount Rushmore's appearance is the gravel below it. It appears as though it was never cleaned up after the heads were carved.

Trekking towards Rapid City, I took another alternate route. The only problem with going off route was that I didn't get the support of Cycle America anymore. They had to stay on route to give the majority of the cyclists support if they needed it. It did make me somewhat nervous, but my bike was in good condition, I had enough food and water, and I only had to ride 35 more miles.

Rapid City was not very biker-friendly. For being fairly large, I thought it would be much more hospitable to our group. We got a lot of honks and funny looks passing through town.

Rapid City was named for Rapid Creek, which flows through town.

Our luggage truck broke down today, so most of the riders had to sit and wait at the school until it arrived.

<u>112 Degrees!</u>

Date: July 14, day 27
Start: Rapid City, SD
End: Interior, SD
Riding time: 4:40
Miles: 85
Maximum speed: 41 mph
Average speed: 18.2 mph
Elevation gain: 2,260 feet
Weather: Sunny and extremely hot, with a temperature of 112!

This was not a good day to get lost.

Jersey Joe took a wrong turn in Scenic, South Dakota, and ended up a long ways from camp. Joe missed a yellow arrow leaving lunch and took off in the wrong direction. After an hour of riding, he finally figured out something was wrong when he saw no arrows or riders. On most other days it wouldn't have been too much of a problem, but there was no relief today. There were very few towns enroute, and even if there was a town, there were no services to be had. The temperature was also unbearably hot.

Joe finally ended up about 30 miles from our destination that night, having already put on 95 miles. He went into a store that he eventually found and luck was on his side. Two Cycle America riders had decided to end their ride early that day and were sightseeing. Joe had noticed them and bummed a ride back to camp in their van. Looking back at the name of the store, he noticed it was called "Angels." He really thought he was in trouble that day and didn't know what he was going to do. I guess someone was looking out for him.

By the 10:00 Scenic lunch spot, the temperature was already in the upper 90s. We had been warned about the heat at the previous night's meeting, but I hadn't expected this.

Getting through such a day requires a lot of willpower and motivation, but I realized the next 35 miles would take more perspiration than inspiration. I also know that people can't drown in their own sweat, so I wasn't too worried!

There were only a few buildings in Scenic, and there were skulls of dead animals hanging above doors. I got out of there as quickly as I could. Scenic wasn't very scenic in my opinion.

Cyclists often have a hard decision to make on such a day. If you ride slower, you conserve your energy and water, but you're in the sun longer. If you ride faster, you use more water and energy, but you're not in the sun as long. I chose to ride a bit harder to try and beat the heat. I still had 35 miles to ride in 112-degree heat and I wasn't looking forward to it. I went through about ten bottles of water from lunch to our ending point. In order to keep us hydrated, Cycle America put extra water out along the route. There were usually three water spots for each day, but we had five today. The company invested in a number of large 30-gallon water jugs that they would simply lock to a wooden sign on the side of the road.

When the biggest highlight of a ride is an overturned trailer home, you know it's a long day.

About ten miles from Interior, South Dakota, I passed a park ranger on the road. He was investigating the over-turned trailer. It had happened the previous day when the semi truck carrying it flipped over. He said that the wind probably had a lot to do with it.

With the temperature so high, I was sure glad I wasn't riding self-contained.

Once arriving in Interior, I got out of the sun as soon as possible, and did my laundry. I couldn't believe that yesterday was one of the best ride days of the trip, and today was one of the worst!

The Badlands

Date: July 15, day 28
Start: Interior, SD
End: Philip, SD
Riding time: 3:35
Miles: 69
Maximum speed: 42 mph
Average speed: 19.3 mph
Elevation gain: 2,260 feet
Weather: Sunny and extremely hot, with temperatures near 100.

Interior is located in an ideal spot for tourists. Even though there is next to nothing in the town, it's near the entrance to the Badlands State Park.

With more than 243,000 acres, the Badlands are simply breathtaking. It was the French Canadian trappers in search of beaver who were the first men to record their impressions of the area. They called the region "bad land to travel across." It's sort of ironic, the land has been so ravaged by wind and water that it has become picturesque.

The Badlands are the bottom of a sea that used to cover the area. Over time, creatures sank to the bottom and eventually became fossilized. When the water receded, the Badlands were exposed to air and sunshine making it into its present-day state.

After a heavy rainfall in the Badlands, red bands stand out. Geologists and paleontologists tell us that these are fossilized soils. A lot can be learned by studying these soils. It is thought that the Badlands hold one of the greatest collections of fossil mammals on earth!

I really enjoyed this day. I had never seen the Badlands before, so I probably stopped 20 times for photos.

Our lunch spot was in Wall, South Dakota.

"The Wall," is a three-mile wide strip of land that separates the lower and upper prairies in the Badlands area. From "The Wall," the town of Wall, South Dakota, got its name.

Wall is perhaps most famous for its drugstore, Wall Drug. During the Great Depression, the owners noticed that the majority of the cars that passed were not stopping. They figured that a lot of the cars going into the Badlands had thirsty folks in them, so they proposed that they put up signs on the highway telling people to come in for free ice water. The Wall Drug Store survived the Depression by offering free ice water to thirsty travelers.

The last 32 miles were very lonely.

The western portion of South Dakota is beautiful with the Black Hills and Badlands, but the farther east you go, the scenery disappears. The landscape becomes desolate and very brown.

South Dakota, like Wisconsin, gives a town's population when entering the city. It was sort of neat to see the varying sizes of towns, but none topped Cottonwood, population 12!

About the only thing in Cottonwood was a little grocery store. One rider from England entered the store to inquire about the sign and to get some food and water.

A woman in the store shot back, "No, the sign is wrong, there are only six of us left."

She went into a long story about how a couple of the residents had died and the others got sick of the place and left. She also claimed that once she sold the place, they'd all be gone. For some reason, I don't think she's going to be able to sell it!

Leaving, the clerk had a parting comment for our rider. She said, "By the way, don't drink the water. It will give you the shits!" He just smiled and left the store shaking his head.

Philip's claim to fame is being the South Dakota home of an Olympic wrestler named Lincoln Mcilravy. Lincoln went to high school here before moving on to the University of Iowa, where he was a national champion. He grew up on a farm just outside of town, and made it known when he was five that he was going to be in the Olympics. He credits his older brothers constantly picking on him as a reason for his success.

His lifelong dream turned into reality when he competed in the 2000 Summer Olympics in Sydney, Australia. He competed in the 152-pound weight class, taking the bronze medal. I was overjoyed when I saw him wrestle, because I had been through the town where it all began for him.

Today was the first time I contemplated what the end in Gloucester would be like. People have asked me if I would ever consider doing another trip like this, and I really don't know. I think the novelty of the whole idea would wear off after the first time. I'm not sure I want to put my body through the pain again. I'm sure if the opportunity came knocking, though, I would at least consider the idea. I would surely take a different route.

The gymnasium was a funny sight in the evening after a ride day. There were bodies scattered everywhere. There usually wasn't too much conversation and most riders walked around like zombies. It was especially bad on this day due to the heat.

I had the same routine every day. When I left from Milwaukee, my dad told me to see and do everything that I could. I took his suggestion literally. After each day's ride, I would quickly shower, grab a bite to eat, set up my camp area, call home, and head for town (if there was one). My first priority was to check my email at the local library. I was able to email about 35 times throughout the summer. I was so excited to see how many I would get each day. It wasn't uncommon to have ten emails in my "inbox." Unfortunately, I wasn't able to individually respond very often due to time constraints. I know some people appreciated my responses, though. I certainly appreciated theirs.

Next I would find the Chamber of Commerce to pick up some brochures. I wanted to learn as much as I could about each area. There were certain days that it was really hard to do all of this, but I managed to do it nine times out of ten.

After returning to camp, I would sit down and write about the day. I would also write postcards. I had certain people I wrote to every day. It was a way for me to combat boredom, think about the people I care about, and keep them informed. I probably wrote two – four a day. Sometimes I tried to take a nap, but usually I couldn't fall asleep because there was too much going on.

And then there was another matter to consider…food!

Looking back, the whole ride revolved around three things: riding your bike, sleeping, and eating as much as you wanted!

Cycle America probably thought we were ravenous vultures (and rude ones at that), but when you're riding 80 miles a day, you need to keep your strength up.

Depending on your weight and biking speed, a cyclist may burn up to 1,000 calories an hour. I used 600 an hour as a gauge, but I'm sure there were times it was a lot higher or lower than that. If you're riding four – five hours a day at 600 calories an hour, that's nearly 3,000 calories right there. Exercise also keeps your metabolism elevated for an extended period of time, even after ceasing, so it wasn't uncommon to consume 6,000 or more calories a day. No matter how much I ate, I was **always** hungry.

Before going on the trip, I told myself to eat properly. That meant eating lots of fruits and vegetables, sport bars and drinks, and other foods that could be quickly absorbed into my body's digestive system. I stuck to my plan for about a week, before I realized how difficult it was to consume 6,000 calories a day. It takes a lot of effort! After week one, I pretty much "grazed" all day long, and ate whatever I wanted. I would eat a solid breakfast, fuel myself up at the lunch spot, and then eat a well-balanced supper. In between I ate a lot of junk! I would often stop at gas stations to buy ice cream or candy. Looking back, I didn't eat that well on the trip, but it didn't matter much, because I was riding 80 miles a day and using all the food I ate as fuel to get me to the next town.

Different riding intensities burn different types of body fuel as well. It's been proven that riding at a lower intensity burns a higher **percentage** of fat, as compared to riding at higher intensities. This can be deceiving, though, because riding at a higher intensity burns more calories in general, so you end up burning more fat calories total. For example, cycling for an hour at a low intensity may burn 350 calories. Of these, about half (175) might be fat calories. Cycling at a high intensity might burn 1,000 calories an hour and 200 of those might be from fat. So, the percentage of fat used is higher at the lower intensity (50 percent as compared to 20 percent), but you still end up burning more fat calories and almost three times as many calories cycling at a higher intensity.

The key to burning fat calories is training your body to do just that. You will naturally burn more fat calories the more fit you get, so start exercising! It often helps to go on a morning ride on an empty stomach (no more than 90 minutes, otherwise you might "bonk"), because it forces your body to turn on its fat-burning system. It usually takes about 20 minutes of cycling before your body taps into its fat stores.

I once read an article about Frank Shorter, a marathon runner, who got tested to see how quickly after starting his exercise his body began utilizing his fat stores. Shorter's body began burning fat the *second* he got on the treadmill!

It's not so important for a touring cyclist, but it's imperative that a pro cyclist eats properly before and during a race, because the pace is usually fast from the beginning. If a touring cyclist eats a heavy meal, they can spend the first hour after eating riding at a slow pace (unless they're climbing a mountain pass) until the meal begins to digest.

I've decided that I could never be a professional cyclist, because I love food way too much. If you're a pro cyclist, you can't even eat a piece of chocolate cake without being considered fat. It's no way to live.

In one of my first bike races, I made the mistake of eating awful the night before. The race was about a five-hour drive from my parents' house in Michigan, so I left the night before and slept in my car at a wayside. Traveling along, I became hungry, so I stopped at a fast-food restaurant and "inhaled" a huge hamburger. I didn't realize I made a mistake until the next day. I spent the first half of the race at the back of the lead pack, struggling to hang on. I finally began to feel better, and actually managed to win the race. It was the first time I've ever won a race (I've won my age group several times), but I wasn't about to reveal my secret on how I did it! Instead of eating a big, greasy hamburger, I should have eaten a meal rich in carbohydrates. Pasta is a favorite pre-race meal for many athletes.

I remember lying down one night at about 10:00 to read a book. As I lay there, my stomach began growling like an angry dog. I couldn't stand it any longer, so I walked a half-mile to town and bought anything I could find. I managed to get lost on the way back, so by the time I got there, I was hungry again! While riding 105 miles in Wisconsin, I ate ice cream five times in one day! It's really been the only time in my life I've been able to eat anything I wanted and not gain any weight. Some people did actually gain weight on the trip, though. If I felt at all guilty about what I consumed, I simply thought about the next day's ride and the feeling went away.

If breakfast was at 7:00, we were lined up at 6:30. If dinner was at 5:00, we were there at 4:30. It was probably a bit rude on our part, but our whole day revolved around it. I guess we were afraid that the food would run out.

If someone had given me a dollar for every time I was asked where and when dinner was on this trip, I'd be a millionaire.

At a rest stop in Washington after climbing Stevens Pass

Some beautiful Montana scenery in the Bitterroot Mountains

"Bobby Kennedy" and I in West Yellowstone, Montana

Getting ready to climb Teton Pass at the Wyoming border

Showing off my farmer's tan at Jewel Cave in South Dakota

Taking a break from the 112-degree heat in the Badlands

Cottonwood, South Dakota, population 12

The Coast-to-Coast 2000 halfway point in Minnesota

A rest stop with a Minnesota family

Some of my family in Menasha, Wisconsin

Asking myself if it was all worth it after a rough day in Michigan

Relaxing by Lake Erie with two weeks left

100 miles to the Atlantic!

Dipping in the Atlantic, and quite possibly the happiest day of my life

Getting ready to party after finishing the tour in Gloucester, Massachusetts

<u>Was it the Water?</u>

Date: July 16, day 29
Start: Philip, SD
End: Fort Pierre, SD
Riding time: 4:50
Miles: 95
Maximum speed: 45 mph
Average speed: 19.7 mph
Elevation gain: 3,430 feet
Weather: Cloudy and cooler, with temperatures in the 60s.

"Don't drink the water. It will give you the shits!"

Those ten magical words reverberated through my head as I sat vomiting in Fort Pierre, South Dakota.

The day started out ordinarily enough, except for a nasty headwind the first 25 miles. Central South Dakota has no protection from the wind. There are endless fields of wheat and clover, but not a single tree to be found. Once I turned east onto South Dakota Highway 34, the wind eased and I was able to fly.

Fifty-four miles into the ride I stopped for lunch. I noticed a big bad storm approaching, so I didn't stay long. It was one of those storms that you see in Oklahoma or Texas coming from miles away. The sky is perfectly clear, but you see this huge mushroom cloud making its way towards you.

I also had an unusual cramping sensation in my stomach, but I didn't think too much of it.

I pedaled quickly for the remainder of the ride. I kept looking behind me to see how much progress the storm was making…it was getting closer.

About six miles from Fort Pierre I broke another spoke. The cramping in my stomach had also gotten worse.

I managed to make it to the Fort Pierre Expo Center without getting wet, but soon I was bent over with pain. Other riders began developing similar symptoms. When the pain and vomiting wouldn't go away, I thought it was a good idea to get some medical help. A few other riders and myself made a trip to the Fort Pierre Medical Center. I was given an IV hookup and some medication to ease my nausea. In all, I spent about three hours there.

Upon investigating the situation, the Fort Pierre Health Department determined that the ailment was thought to be viral and not food poisoning. They also ruled out the bad water, as they said we probably didn't drink enough of it to get sick. They did feel that it could have been a combination of all three factors, though. About half of the riders developed similar symptoms over the next few days. Food poisoning would have lasted a day until the contaminated food was out of our systems, but the fact that the illness lasted for several days confirmed the theory of the sickness being viral.

Nevertheless, maybe I shouldn't have eaten those runny eggs this morning!

I was very fortunate to have finished the day. My ride-every-mile goal was almost brought to an abrupt end, and there would have been nothing I could have done about it. I was also lucky that the next day was a scheduled day off so I could recuperate. In the end, I guess I have to thank a big bad storm for pushing me to Fort Pierre.

Fort Pierre is the oldest continuous settlement in the state of South Dakota. Almost 250 years ago, French explorers first discovered the land along the Missouri River. Its central location on the river was a strong attraction to early explorers, settlers, and traders.

On my day off, I also got a chance to tour the South Dakota state Capitol in Pierre. Pierre is a rather small town for a state Capital, but it was pretty, nonetheless. Pierre was also voted as the tenth best small town in America in 2000.

The Capitol Building was constructed in 1910. It's made from limestone, fieldstone, and marble. The original cost was just over one million dollars, but its estimated value today is 58 million!

Little did I know, but the "fun" was just beginning for me.

"Mighty Rivers"
South Dakota/Minnesota

<u>A Day of Infamy</u>

Date: July 18, day 31
Start: Fort Pierre, SD
End: Miller, SD
Riding time: 6:50
Miles: 95
Maximum speed: 25 mph
Average speed: 13.9 mph
Elevation gain: 3,000 feet
Weather: Cloudy, rainy, and cool, with a 25-mph headwind, and
          temperatures near 50.

In his book, "It's Not About the Bike," Lance Armstrong says, "Pro cycling is so hard that you can't even stop to take a 'piss'."

I can't think of a better quote under the circumstances.

Cycling *is* a hard sport…very hard.

July 18, 2000, was unequivocally the worst day I've ever spent on a bike…possibly the worst day of my life, period. There was absolutely no reason to be riding this day. It was the only day the entire trip that I didn't want to ride. It took every ounce of my strength to finish.

Before I went to bed last night, I could hear the rain pounding on the metal roof of the Expo Center. I hoped and prayed that it would stop by daybreak…it didn't.

The weather was absolutely deplorable. The temperature didn't get above 50 and it never stopped drizzling all day. The rainy weather also turned the roads into a quagmire. Add to the mix a 25-mph headwind and it became an impossible day…almost.

It should have been a pretty ride along the Missouri River, but I can honestly say I didn't look at it once…I didn't care. I was too busy pedaling with my head down concentrating on the job at hand. I still hadn't fully recovered from my sickness, either, so that made matters worse.

Eighteen miles out, I got a flat tire. After changing it, I realized that I had packed only one spare tube (I usually pack two). It was just another thing to add to the list on an already difficult day.

At this point I remember slouching over my bike for a minute and asking myself, "What in the hell are you doing out here?" I still don't know if I can tell you the answer.

Cyclists hate headwinds and this was a nasty one. I was in my lowest gear (39 x 25) and it still wasn't enough. It's very demoralizing to a biker when your heart feels ready to explode, and you look down to search for a lower gear and it's not there. Going 12 mph didn't help the morale, either.

Surprisingly, I didn't feel too bad physically, but I soon found another potential problem. I hadn't taken into account the stiff headwind at breakfast, so I quickly realized I might not have enough energy to make it to lunch. There were no towns enroute, so I was in serious trouble. Normally after a good breakfast, 50 miles on a bike is no problem, but this was no ordinary day.

For every problem I found a solution. Somebody was definitely looking out for me.

After traveling 30 miles, a van pulled up along side me. It was a couple of riders who had chosen not to ride that day because they still hadn't recovered from their sickness. They gave me all the food they had so I could continue. I'm convinced that without their help, I wouldn't have made it.

I was also underdressed once again. I was wearing a rain jacket, but I should have worn tights and booties.

After four long hours and 50 miles of riding, I reached the lunch spot. Fearing hypothermia, I didn't stay long. Taking off, I noticed a sign that Cycle America had painted on the road that said, "Miller – 45 miles." My heart sank. I thought I couldn't possibly make it that far, but I trudged on.

I kept thinking it was all a bad dream, and that there was no way a day could be so ugly. It had to change, but I knew it wouldn't. I tried making excuses for the weather and the difficulty of the day, but I didn't have time for that. If I used my energy that way, I wouldn't have the energy to deal with what I really needed to deal with: getting to Miller, South Dakota, as fast as I could.

Lance Armstrong knows all about making excuses. When his right testicle became slightly swollen in 1996, he made excuses; when his nipples became sore, he made excuses; when he had to drop out of the 1996 Tour de France due to bronchitis, a sore throat, and lower-back pain, he made excuses; when he coughed up blood and had migraines, he made excuses. I wasn't going to make excuses.

The next 45 miles were perhaps the longest of my life.

For the first 25 miles, I was in la-la land, not knowing who or where I was (like a dream). It was the one time on the trip that I was afraid to be alone. I thought about waiting for someone at lunch, but I just wanted to get done.

Cycle America made a few route changes at lunch, so I wasn't even sure I was going in the right direction. The roads were so desolate and rough, that I thought I had to be going the wrong way. I didn't see one car in those 25 miles. I kept wondering how long it would take before my legs would seize up and quit working.

It was here that I wondered what my family and friends were doing back home. I wished I could have seen them…or better yet, they could have seen what I was going through. If there had been a phone around, I would have called and told them to think about me. I guess I wanted someone to feel sorry for me. (I told one of my sisters that it's the only day in my life where I've ever felt sorry for myself.) Even though they had no idea what was happening to me, I imagined they did, and it helped me make it through. My mother recently told me that she prayed for me every day; I know the power of prayer, because it got me through this day.

At mile 75 I turned north on South Dakota Highway 45 and the wind eased somewhat. I remember letting out a huge "whoop" when I reached 15 mph, because I was so happy. I also remember chuckling to myself as I realized no one was probably within five miles of me.

With 15 miles to go I stopped the service van and got a spare tube. I knew I was too cold to change another flat anyway, but my stress level went way down.

Three miles later another support vehicle stopped to check in with me. They could see my pain, but also my determination. The van was full of riders who had cashed it in for the day and I can't say I blamed them.

Needing a boost to get me to Miller, one of Cycle America's staff members put her arm around me and said, "Rich, there's a nice warm school waiting for you in 12 miles." Those 12 magical words hit me like a rock and gave me the gumption to ride again.

I don't know if I could have made it without the chocolate chip cookies they gave me, either!

A person must have the motivation to overcome things that get in your way. A lot of people get so close to success, and then give up. I wasn't going to do that. At this point I knew I would make it to Miller, even if I had to walk my bike the 12 miles. I also realize that motivation won't take you very far if you don't have the legs to get you there, and today I had the legs.

Soon I entered the city limits of Miller, and I began to cry. I think it was from realizing the monumental task I had just completed. I was so tired that I never wanted to ride again, but I also felt like I had just won the lottery. I still don't know how I made it. It was definitely a test from God.

Because it was so cold, I used a lot of calories. I estimate that I burned about 10,000 calories on this day.

I'm also convinced that had I not trained so hard, there's no way I would have made it to Miller. There were about six times I felt like quitting, but I knew I couldn't. I remember asking myself several times during the day, if this is what it feels like to "look death in the eyes."

When I pulled into the school, I could barely get off my bike. My body was going through a phase called "bonking." Bonking is a slang term for when a person's body runs completely out of energy. All of my body's stored glycogen was used up.

A couple of riders who had chosen not to ride that day, helped me get off my bike and gave me some quick energy in the form of soda and cookies. I had to sit with my back against a wall for quite some time to regain my composure. My hands and feet were cramping, I was hallucinating, my head was pounding, my legs felt like jelly, my speech was slurred, and I felt like I could have taken an eight-hour nap! Other than that, I felt fine! Finally after 20 minutes (and the sugar began to circulate through my body), I was helped to my feet and started to feel normal again.

The first time I "bonked" was during my first-ever-competitive ski race, so I was "young and stupid." I was feeling so good during the first part that I completely forgot to eat properly. With about 30 minutes yet to race, I noticed I was having a hard time focusing and skiing. I soon began hallucinating and had to stop. I began cramping and vomiting in the middle of the ski trail. I figured I would have to drop out, but I stood there for a few minutes and managed to regain my strength. The last six miles were extremely difficult, but I struggled to the finish line. As bad as I felt in that ski race, I felt much **worse** on that cold, rainy day in South Dakota.

After getting a hot shower and something more to eat, I called my dad back in Michigan and told him the horror story of the day. He had just picked up the local paper and told me that my buddy, Tom, from Wisconsin, had written a sport brief about me. It said how I had battled my way through a viral sickness to keep my goal of riding every mile intact. When I heard this, I began to cry again. I had to fight back the tears so others wouldn't see. I felt that if I hadn't ridden every mile this day, I not only would be letting myself down, but the whole community that had given me the support back home. They were all counting on me.

I really don't know what this day did to me, but it changed my life forever. Not a day passes I don't think about it.

People have asked me what I thought about. I can't really say I remember. I know I did a lot of singing and praying, that's for sure.

One thing I did think about was a conference I attended in the summer of 1998 in Kenosha, Wisconsin. I got the opportunity to hear a speaker named Murray Banks. Murray was a world champion cross-country skier in his age group who said that too many people worry about things they don't have to. To avoid too much worry, he assigns every situation a number between one and ten. If the situation doesn't need much attention, assign it a low number. If it deserves more attention, you might assign it a higher number.

He gave the following example: if you get a flat tire on your car, give it a two. You can change it, or if you don't know how, someone else does. If you get a flat tire on the way to work, assign it a five.

You can still change it, but now you're under a bit more pressure. If you get a flat tire in downtown Detroit at midnight, that one might deserve a ten!

July 18, 2000, will long be remembered in my mind as a ten.

Olympic runner Wilma Rudolph once said, "No matter what accomplishments you make, somebody helps you."

I have too many people to thank for helping me this day. If you took any one of them away, I probably wouldn't have made it.

<u>The Home of Laura</u>

Date: July 19, day 32
Start: Miller, SD
End: DeSmet, SD
Riding time: 4:10
Miles: 79
Maximum speed: 27 mph
Average speed: 19 mph
Elevation gain: 1,120 feet
Weather: Cloudy and cool, with temperatures in the 60s.

In cycling you need a good team and today I had one.

Lance Armstrong has admitted that winning the Tour de France wouldn't have been possible without his team. They put him in position to win the Tour by protecting him during crucial stages of the race.

If you watch the Tour, you'll see a number of tactics used to protect the team leader. First off, rarely will you see Armstrong riding in the wind. Instead he'll be behind teammates conserving energy. It's estimated that cyclists can save up to 30 percent of their energy "drafting" behind others. Drafting is positioning oneself behind another rider's back wheel (in most cases, depending on the direction of the wind). In essence, it's like a big vacuum cleaner sucking you along. The lead riders are working harder because they're breaking the wind. Drafting is used in car racing much the same way.

In the mountains, Armstrong's teammates sacrifice their chances to ensure his victory. You'll see them setting a high pace at the front in order to rid Armstrong of his rivals. Slowly, one by one they peel off the front and struggle to finish the day. To the non-cyclist it doesn't seem fair, but it's a very common team tactic. It makes more sense to work for the strongest rider on a team to make sure he wins. As a token of his appreciation Armstrong helps his teammates in other races.

Great riders cannot exist without their lesser-talented teammates. Most people don't realize how much protection is given to the top riders. I notice it mainly when watching a mountainous race. First you'll see the top stars come zooming by, and then many minutes later, you'll see the lesser-known riders come struggling by trying to get to the end in one piece. I feel so bad for them, because they do a lot of the work, and many of them never reap the rewards for doing so.

Armstrong's main objective is to stay out of trouble in the early stages, and then surge when the time is right.

A number of excellent riders have never won a race because they're on poor teams. If a star rider is isolated in a small group with no teammates, it's a dangerous situation because that's when others will attack. Often in a race, the best rider doesn't win, but the best team certainly does. Good teams know that the need to outsmart their opponent is far more important than overpowering them.

Another tactic used in cycling is "blocking." Blocking is when a team positions itself into a group that is chasing one of their teammates up the road. You'll see them sitting in the pack not doing any work at all. They have no obligation to help because their teammate is ahead of the race. The teams chasing the lead rider don't like it one bit, but there's nothing they can do about it.

For instance, if I was on a nine-man team in a race, and about halfway through I attacked and went off the front of the pack, I would expect the other eight riders on my team to help me win by ***not*** helping the other riders "chase me down." My teammates would "block" the other riders from reaching me, thus the term. In a pack, often riders take turns being the lead rider to break the wind, but in this situation my teammates would not be expected to. They'd actually try to slow down the pace as much as possible in the pack, so I could gain as much time as I could.

An unwritten rule in pro cycling is having to put in your time before being successful. The 1996 Paris-Roubaix was a classic example.

Veteran Belgian Johann Museeuw and Italians Gianluca Bortolami and Andrea Tafi were alone approaching the finish. All three of the riders were on the same team, but since Museeuw was a polished veteran and the other two were not, he was allowed to win. When the trio knew they were going to stay clear of the other riders, the team director made the decision.

You could see Museeuw's two teammates were visibly upset, but there was nothing they could do about it. With 15 kilometers to go Museeuw got a flat tire. Bortolami and Tafi could have ridden away to victory, but they waited for Museeuw and he was victorious in the end.

If the other two hadn't waited for or allowed Museeuw to win, they would have been fired from the team and would have had trouble finding another one.

Three years later in the 1999 Paris-Roubaix, Andrea Tafi got his opportunity to win. He couldn't have done it without the help of Johann Museeuw.

I've found the best way to learn cycling tactics is to watch pro-cycling videos. I have over 50 that I watch over and over…and over again! By doing this, I'm able to watch the best riders in the world without leaving the confines of my own home. Then when I go out for a group ride with my riding club, I put the strategies I've learned into practice. Most of the racing terms and examples I have included in this day-by-day recap I've learned from watching these videos.

After yesterday's devilish ride, today was a piece of cake. I chose to ride with a group to recover a bit. I rode with Jersey Joe and a few others. I was able to draft behind Joe and relax the whole day.

DeSmet, South Dakota, was made famous when Laura Ingalls Wilder used the town as a setting for six of her "Little House" books. They all took place between 1879 and 1894 in DeSmet.

DeSmet is named for Father DeSmet, a Jesuit missionary who spent his life among the Indians. There is a beautiful statue honoring him in the center of town.

A New Game

Date: July 20, day 33
Start: DeSmet, SD
End: Watertown, SD
Riding time: 3:45
Miles: 60
Maximum speed: 27 mph
Average speed: 16 mph
Elevation gain: 1,770 feet
Weather: Mostly cloudy and cooler, with temperatures in the
mid 60s.

I thought of a new game today!

Each day I would search for new things to get me through. If I had an exceptionally long day, I would break the ride into percentages and segments, so it wouldn't seem quite as long. You can't sit on the starting line and say to yourself, "I've got to ride 80 miles today." Instead, think to yourself, "I have four rides of twenty miles each." This way, you don't get intimidated by what seems an impossible distance. I knew that if I could make it to lunch (there I go again…talking about food), I wouldn't have too much further to go.

I also played with my cycling computer a lot. I was constantly looking at it to decipher the facts. I could look at my current, average, and maximum speed, riding time, my elevation, and the temperature. Sometimes it felt like my life *was* that computer. I don't know what I would have done without it. Sometimes it ran my ride too much, though. I'm sure I missed things along the way because I was looking at that "stupid" thing.

The day got long due to a rather nasty headwind, but the scenery and greenness started to come back. For the first time on the trip I saw green fields of corn and soybeans. I never thought I'd be so happy to see a cornfield.

The headwind was easier to deal with because I knew I wouldn't be on my bike for seven hours, it was warmer, and it wasn't raining.

I was also entering an area of the United States that is made up of small towns. I forgot how nice it was to cycle through them since it had been so long since I had done that.

I entitled the game the "License Plate Game." I'm sure others have tried it, so I take no responsibility for being its founder. If it doesn't work for you, you just need to appreciate why I did it!

As a car would approach me from behind, I would get ready to read the license plate, attempting to see what state the vehicle was from, and what the numbers on it were. You'd be surprised at how many I was able to read. Since we were mainly on back roads today, the cars were traveling a bit slower, so it was easier. It also got my mind off that computer!

So...if I wasn't missing things due to my computer, it was because I was looking at license plates.

Every so often we had a chance to visit hospitals, nursing homes, and schools. In Bryant, South Dakota, a few of the riders went into a nursing home to visit the patients. After telling one of them about the bike trip, a 101-year-old woman with a cute smile and no teeth yelled out, "I want to ride my bike!" She said all of this as she punched the air with her fist. She could barely walk, but you have to appreciate her spunk.

After nine days of riding, this was my last full day in South Dakota. Those nine days were filled with contrast, misery, pain, heat, cold, rain, and pleasure. I often tell people that South Dakota was not only my favorite state, but also my least favorite. I had mixed emotions about leaving, but I guess I was ready for it.

Watertown, South Dakota, was the first Watertown we stayed in. The other was in New York. Watertown, South Dakota, is actually named after its New York counterpart. The original city of Watertown was abandoned after grasshoppers destroyed the crops. Watertown came about when the railroad extended its lines.

It's also famous for being the hometown of Terry Redlin, perhaps America's best-known wildlife artist. If you're ever in Watertown, South Dakota, a must to see is The Redlin Art Center. Since opening in 1997, nearly a million people have visited it!

Watertown was the largest town we visited since Rapid City, but was more biker-friendly.

<u>Which Way do I Go?</u>

Date: July 21, day 34
Start: Watertown, SD
End: Montevideo, MN
Riding time: 4:05
Miles: 85
Maximum speed: 40 mph
Average speed: 20.8 mph
Elevation gain: 1,170 feet
Weather: Cloudy and cool, with temperatures in the mid 60s.

Soybeans!

It's funny…this ride was one of the fastest and flattest of the summer, but I missed the mountains! You have to work so hard going up and down them, that it really keeps you focused on the day.

Halfway through the day's 85-mile jaunt, I entered into Minnesota, my sixth state. Cycle America had put balloons and signs on the road to symbolize the halfway point of the Coast-to-Coast ride. They even painted a sign on the road. Instead of the Continental Divide, it was called the "Ride Divide." It had an arrow pointing west that read, "Pacific," and another pointing east saying, "Atlantic." I didn't consider turning around and going back to the Pacific, but it was a rather emotional time. They say some Veterans have "Nam" flashbacks when thinking back to their days in Vietnam. Well, I had "Coast-to-Coast" flashbacks when remembering the first half of the ride.

About 20 miles from the finish, I passed through Madison, Minnesota. The Scandinavian and German people settled the area permanently. One delicacy they brought with them was Lutefisk. Lutefisk is made from codfish prepared according to their ethnic tradition. Many people refuse to eat it because of its appearance and smell, but others simply love it. Madison is known as "Lutefisk Capital USA." I guess that would explain the smell when I pedaled through town.

Our first overnight town in Minnesota was Montevideo. Montevideo is located in southwestern Minnesota where the Chippewa and Minnesota rivers converge.

Montevideo, Minnesota, is named after the capital of Uruguay, South America. Over the years, representatives of both cities have exchanged visits.

In 1949, the South American Montevideo presented its North American partner a statue of Jose Artigas, a hero of Uruguayan Independence. This eleven-foot bronze statue overlooks the downtown area.

Lance Armstrong also took another step towards winning his second Tour de France this day. He won the stage 19 individual time trial by 26 seconds over German Jan Ullrich. The individual time trial is called the "race of truth," because it's man versus man, one on one. There are no teams to help; it's just you and your bike going as fast as you possibly can. Riders usually start two minutes apart, so they don't have the benefit of drafting (which is illegal in a time trial anyway). Armstrong won all three time trials in the 2000 Tour, reconfirming that he was the best in the world.

In a time trial, it's extremely important to be as aerodynamic as possible. Since most wind drag in cycling occurs from one's own body, keeping a low profile on the bike is the best way to combat this. In most cases, pro riders are separated by mere seconds over the course of their event. You will see them wearing "funky" skin suits and using specially shaped bikes that cut through the wind with more efficiency.

The difference between Lance Armstrong and his rivals is not their lack of strength or knowledge, but rather their lack of will. No other cyclist in the world has more will than Lance Armstrong. It takes a lot of will to train six or seven hours a day for days on end, something that Lance does quite often. There are other cyclists on the professional circuit who have more talent than Armstrong, but they are unable to motivate themselves to the level that he does.

Physically, Lance Armstrong is a freak of nature. He's one in maybe ten million because the amount of fatigue-causing lactic acid produced by his cycling muscles is only one-fourth that of his competitors. There are very few people on earth with his ability.

Lactic acid is a waste product produced by your muscles during very intense exercise. The acid interferes with the muscles' ability to turn food into energy. Lactic acid also draws in water, which lowers blood volume. This makes it harder to deliver oxygen and impossible to sustain a hard effort for long.

You will especially notice lactic acid (in biking) when climbing for a sustained period of time (or on a short intense climb) or during a long sprint. All riders feel the pain of lactic acid, but how your body deals with it is the key. When I get that burning feeling in my legs, I totally block out the pain and keep going. I know that once I get to the top of the mountain, or across the finish line, the negative feeling will go away. I've noticed that as the years have gone by, I've gotten better at dealing with the effects of lactic acid, not only physically, but mentally as well.

<u>Soy Beans, Corn, and Sugar Beets</u>

Date: July 22, day 35
Start: Montevideo, MN
End: Hutchinson, MN
Riding time: 4:20
Miles: 80
Maximum speed: 23 mph
Average speed: 18.5 mph
Elevation gain: 1,040 feet
Weather: Mostly sunny and hot, with temperatures in the 80s.

The scenery in the Midwest is very serene. It's definitely not as breathtaking as the mountains out West, but it gives a person a feeling of relaxation because of all the greenness.

I counted nine different combinations of crops. There might be corn on the left and soybeans on the right, or sugar beets on the left and corn on the right, etc.

With only 1,040 feet of elevation gain, this was our second flattest day. I can go for an hour ride in Rhinelander and climb that much.

Before I left on the trip, I was curious about being chased by dogs. It's really not something that most cyclists think about, but they should. If you don't deal with it the proper way, it can be a potentially dangerous situation.

While riding my usual biking route in Michigan, a small dog came running out at me. It seemed like he would sit and wait in the bushes for me to appear and then attack. Once when he charged out of the bushes, I had nowhere to go, so I ran into him. I managed to keep my bike upright, but I was lucky. I don't remember having too many other problems with him after that.

What should you do if chased by a dog? I'm sure you've heard a lot of advice, but you need to stay calm. I often try to sprint away if I can, because I know I can pedal a lot faster than they can run. Other times I give them a squirt with my water bottle. This usually does the trick, but you're wasting your drink this way. I think you need to avoid using your feet to kick or a frame pump to hit with. This will only hurt the dog and agitate him even more. Usually a loud yell will be enough to keep him from chasing you.

I tell you all of this because today I got chased for the first time all summer. It happened on two separate occasions, but I managed to come away from both instances unscathed.

I really didn't see too many wild animals on this trip. Looking back, that's the one thing I was most disappointed about. Obviously, it wasn't Cycle America's fault, though. There are times in Wisconsin that I fear for my life when going on a morning ride, due to all the deer running across the road in front of me. I expected to see deer and other small animals on the trip, but I also wanted to see bear, buffalo, and moose. Unfortunately, I didn't get to see too many animals in their natural state.

Most of the time our lunch stop was nowhere in particular. Cycle America usually picked the most convenient spot for us, often in a park or on a side road, but on this day we got a special treat. We had lunch at an animal farm! Since I grew up around a lot of animals, I really enjoyed it. The family made us feel right at home and I was starting to enjoy the Midwestern hospitality.

The remainder of the ride was spent cycling by corn and soybeans fields.

Hutchinson, Minnesota, was a very nice overnight town. Singers John, Asa, and Judson Hutchinson are credited with founding the town. The three brothers heard of Minnesota from a friend in New England, so they took off west with the intention of establishing a community. They met a surveyor who helped them select a suitable spot, and they staked their claim.

The End of Jesse James

Date: July 23, day 36
Start: Hutchinson, MN
End: Northfield, MN
Riding time: 4:45
Miles: 88
Maximum speed: 37 mph
Average speed: 18.5 mph
Elevation gain: 2,400 feet
Weather: Mostly sunny and hot, with temperatures in the 80s.

My day of cycling started calm and stayed that way.

After five weeks, I was becoming accustomed to life on the road, and I liked it. Maybe it was because I knew I'd see family and friends within the week. The roads were also extremely good. There was a lot of new blacktop, so it quickly made me forget about all the rough roads of the West. Since entering Minnesota, the roads were much better.

Just like Devils Tower, my destination was the focus of my ride. I wanted to get to Northfield to view some American history.

Jesse James was perhaps the most notorious bank robber in history, but it wasn't until the people of Northfield, Minnesota, stood up for their rights, that he was finally stopped.

On September 7, 1876, the James' Gang approached the downtown area of Northfield, but were thwarted in their efforts by the brave townspeople, who armed themselves with all available guns and ammunition.

Each weekend after Labor Day, Northfield relives and re-enacts that fateful day to celebrate the bravery of its townspeople who stood up to the James' Gang. The Defeat of Jesse James Days attracts over 100,000 people to town in September. Some day I'd like to go back to Northfield over Labor Day Weekend and take in the re-enactment.

Two of the finest liberal arts colleges in the country are located in Northfield, Carleton College (1866) and St. Olaf College (1874).

Many of the riders spent the next day off on a bus trip to the Mall of America in Minneapolis. I decided against it because I had remembered our last bus trip to the national parks, and I didn't want to be tired for the next day's ride. In retrospect, I probably should have gone, but shopping isn't my forte.

I spent my day off cleaning my bike. It's very important to keep a clean bike, especially after riding in wet or dirty conditions. If your gears get full of dirt, oil, or other debris, it will wear them out quicker. Your chain and other parts will also see more wear. I tried to clean my bike once a week on the trip. Cleaning your bike is like cleaning your toilet. If you do it on a regular basis, it's an easy job. If you wait too long, it's an utterly disgusting chore!

I thought my bike held up extremely well. From the experiences I've had, the more you pay for a bike, the longer it will last. My first bike was a $500, aluminum-frame road bike. It served a very good purpose for me, as I was a poor college student, so it was about the only thing that I could afford. It had decent components (gears, shifters, brakes, etc.), but it wasn't top of the line. The second bike I bought was the one I used on Coast-to-Coast 2000. I paid about $1,000 for it, so it was quite a step up from my previous bike. It had a steel frame, which is slightly heavier, but it had much better components. I could see a big difference with the shifting. It was a lot faster, and didn't make as much noise. I also got a better "ride" from my second road bike. About a year after finishing my trip, I invested in another bike. This time I went with a carbon-fiber bike, and paid about $2,500 for it. Although expensive, I absolutely love it. It's extremely light (3.5 pounds for the frame), but also durable. Since I've ridden three different types of frame material, I can vouch for carbon. It gives me the smoothest ride, and is very appealing to look at. Unlike aluminum and steel, carbon frames are molded in one single piece, so there are no sloppy weld marks.

I think the most important thing to look for when purchasing a bike is good components. They're the first thing that will wear out and give you problems, so spending a little more money will give you components made to last for longer miles. It is possible to buy a cheaper-framed bike, and then install better components (to save some money), but I do not recommend this.

Department store bikes are not meant to be fixed; they're meant to be thrown away. I *guarantee* you that if you buy an $89 department-store bike, within a week (depending on how much you ride) you'll have problems with it. It's much better to spend a little more money initially.

It's a personal decision on how much you want to spend on a bike, but with each new, more-expensive bike that I've bought, I've noticed a *huge* difference in how they've preformed. With each bike I bought, I thought it was the greatest bike in the world, until I purchased the next one! I'm quite certain that if I upgraded to a more expensive bike (yes…they're out there!), I'd be even happier with it. I've seen bikes priced as high as $6,000. I think it all depends on your goals, and the amount of miles you ride.

Many people and I have a difference of opinion when it comes to biking. They think I should get new carpeting or linoleum for my house; I think I should purchase a new bike!

Having said all of this, it's still vital to realize that it's more important how you train, as compared to what type of bike you're riding.

"Heartland Patchwork"
Wisconsin

Entering Wisconsin

Date: July 26, day 38
Start: Northfield, MN
End: Pepin, WI
Riding time: 3:40
Miles: 67
Maximum speed: 37 mph
Average speed: 18.3 mph
Elevation gain: 2,020 feet
Weather: Cloudy with rain showers, with temperatures in the
upper 80s.

Wisconsin!

There was a very special feeling entering into Wisconsin, my home state. While others had their chance throughout the trip, this was my chance to brag and boast.

Wisconsin is nicknamed the Badger State for the early miners who dug holes in the hills.

Two weeks ago I had made arrangements to visit with family and friends during the week. At one point I would be able to visit with people I knew for five straight days. It really kept me motivated and focused on riding, and it gave me something to look forward to.

Several months before the official start of my ride, I told people that I was already depressed about the end of the ride, and it hadn't even begun yet. That's how I sort of felt entering this week. I was so looking forward to seeing familiar faces, but I was also dreading that ferry ride across Lake Michigan later in the week. I knew it would be a big let-down.

Shortly after starting, I developed some pain in my right Achilles Tendon. It's not an area to "mess around with," so I took it easy pedaling. I think it was just some tendonitis from overuse.

Most of the time Cycle America routed us on vehicle highways, but today we got to ride on a bike path! The Cannon Valley Trail is an abandoned railway about 20 miles long, connecting Cannon Falls, to Red Wing, Minnesota. It's very well maintained and reminded me of a tropical rain forest. We would be without service for the duration of the trail, but I was now able to change a flat in my sleep, so I wasn't worried.

Cannon Falls is the home of Cycle America.

After crossing over the Mississippi River and stopping for a photo at the border, I was able to ride on Wisconsin Highway 35. It was absolutely beautiful, as it took us parallel to the river. I highly recommend a trip to western Wisconsin to ride on it.

The town of Pepin, Wisconsin, has as much history as any town in the United States. It was here that Laura Ingalls Wilder was born. Laura's first book, "Little House in the Big Woods," was set in Pepin of the 1870s.

I'm a little afraid to admit it, but I am a huge fan of the TV version of "Little House on the Prairie." I have seen *every* episode and can tell you within five minutes of the beginning what the show is about.

Pierre and Jean Pepin, who came here from the St. Lawrence River region in Canada, first explored Pepin. The presence of these two men resulted in the name Pepin being used.

The city grew around the lake with the same name, and it was thought that it would one day grow as large as Milwaukee. Luckily for the residents, it did not. The area's peaceful, rural attraction has made it into a tourist spot. Pepin is an awesome place to visit in the fall because of the colorful foliage.

All I could think about that night was finally getting to see someone I knew the following day, my sister, Kathy's in-laws, who would meet me in Osseo, Wisconsin.

Familiar Faces!

Date: July 27, day 39
Start: Pepin, WI
End: Osseo, WI
Riding time: 3:15
Miles: 63
Maximum speed: 48 mph
Average speed: 19.4 mph
Elevation gain: 3,500 feet
Weather: Cloudy, warm, and rainy, with temperatures in the 70s.

The toughest 63 miles of the trip…hardly.

At the previous night's meeting our router told us that this would be the toughest portion of the trip, so I was expecting the worse. But after going up and over the Rockies and Tetons, this was a "piece of cake." Although the day was among the top five in elevation gained, it wasn't by any stretch too difficult to handle.

The climbs were short, but steep. Out West the climbs are long, but more gradual. It takes two different types of riders for these climbs. The longer, more gradual climbs favor the endurance rider; the rider who can go at a steady pace that will break the legs of his opponents. I prefer these types of climbs. The steeper, shorter climbs would favor power. These climbs are more difficult because you can never get into a rhythm. You constantly have to get out of the saddle to keep up your cadence.

Entering Osseo, I got caught in a nasty thunderstorm. We were supposed to stay at a campground, but that had flooded. We ended up staying at the local high school instead.

It was there that I met my sister's in-laws. We went to a local park to converse, and then they took me to the "Norski Nook" for dinner. With their advice, I tried a famous Norwegian specialty called "Lefsa." It's a tortilla that tastes like potato. We also had the "Nook's" famous homemade pie. I'm guessing they had 20 different kinds, and most of the riders would agree it was very tasty. It's a must if you are near Osseo.

Osseo is a Norwegian community, but the name is Indian. A story says that as the Indians broke over the hills coming into town their chief said, "Ah-See-Oh," describing the beauty of the view.

Even though I live in Wisconsin, I had never been to either Pepin or Osseo, so it was nice to visit them.

<u>Cranberry Country</u>

Date: July 28, day 40
Start: Osseo, WI
End: Wisconsin Rapids, WI
Riding time: 4:35
Miles: 92
Maximum speed: 35 mph
Average speed: 20.1 mph
Elevation gain: 1,820 feet
Weather: Mostly sunny and warm, with temperatures in the 70s.

More friends!

Unlike Pepin and Osseo, I had been to Wisconsin Rapids, Wisconsin, before. The Rhinelander Hodags are in the same conference as the Red Raiders, so I'm quite familiar with the area.

Located on the Wisconsin River (the same river that flows through Rhinelander), it's known for its paper production, dairy farms, and cranberry marshes. Wood County has the largest inland acreage of cranberry marshes in the world.

About three weeks ago, I got an email from one of my former students who was wondering if her dad could take her and a friend down to Wisconsin Rapids to visit with me. Her dad and I teach at the same school in Rhinelander. I met them at the school, and spent the afternoon with them at the local park. It was my second day in a row seeing people I knew. Tomorrow would be the culmination of the celebration, though. My parents, three of my sisters and their families, and my good friend Tom were coming to Menasha, Wisconsin, to visit with me. They were planning a picnic for me and the other riders. I always knew that my mom was a good cook, but even I was surprised at what they brought.

I also visited a cancer ward on this day. My aunt and uncle died from the disease, and my mom has breast cancer, so I know what it's like to go through it; it's such a devastating disease. I think that's why I took a liking to Lance Armstrong so much. When he was diagnosed with testicular cancer in 1996, doctors gave him a 30 percent chance of survival, as he developed two lesions in his brain and twelve golf-ball-sized tumors in his abdomen and lungs. The lesions were successfully removed, and after chemotherapy he was finally given a clean bill of health a year later. After he recovered, his doctor told him that his case was the **worst** he had ever seen, and in fact he thought his chance of survival was zero. Six years later, Lance is still cancer-free.

Before he was diagnosed, Armstrong has admitted he was a brash, arrogant individual, but cancer changed him, both physically and mentally.

During his cancer, Lance lost all of his muscle mass. When it grew back, it came back differently. Instead of being bulky and heavy, it came back smaller and sleeker. He ended up losing about 20 pounds during the ordeal. He returned to competition in 1998 and promptly took fourth at the Tour of Spain and the World Championships. He would win the Tour de France for the first time the following summer.

Armstrong bounced back so quickly after his cancer, that during one of his first training camps, one of his teammates was heard saying, "Lance, you're killing everybody and you had cancer!"

Armstrong has said that he could not have won the Tour if he hadn't had cancer. Not only was he lighter physically (which is good for the mountains), but he was also stronger mentally. He's also said that if he had to chose between winning the Tour and having cancer, he would pick having cancer, because cancer patients are the real survivors. He doesn't know why he got the illness, but it did wonders for him, and he wouldn't want to walk away from it.

I thought it was really ironic that the French media accused Armstrong of using drugs. When he found out about it, he calmly replied, "After putting drugs into my body that were so toxic the nurses had to use gloves, why would I want to poison my body again?" Armstrong has **never** tested positive for any illegal drugs.

When asked what kind of performance-enhancing drug he's on, Lance responds: "What am I on? I'm on my bike busting my ass six hours a day. What are you on?" The media thought his comeback was a miracle, to which Armstrong replied, "It was."

Earlier in the day, I was able to cycle on some very nice Wisconsin-country back roads. I also was able to see deer, turkeys, geese, and the Wisconsin state bird…the mosquito!

When I stopped for lunch, I was "swarmed under" by mosquitoes and biting gnats. I spent more time swatting at them, than I did eating, so I left as quickly as I could to avoid getting eaten alive.

Later that evening we had a weigh-in at the school. I wasn't doing the trip to lose weight, but some of the other riders were definitely watching their caloric intake. A couple riders from Washington ended up losing 25 pounds each. I stayed the same.

At bedtime, another rider told me there was a young girl out in the parking lot that claimed to be from Rhinelander. She turned out to be the niece of one of my good friends. Her aunt knew she'd be down in Wisconsin Rapids visiting a friend, so she told her that I would be there, too. I think unexpected guests are always the best.

Family Reunion

Date: July 28, day 41
Start: Wisconsin Rapids, WI
End: Menasha, WI
Riding time: 5:40
Miles: 105
Maximum speed: 35 mph
Average speed: 18.6 mph
Elevation gain: 2,130 feet
Weather: Cloudy, cool, and rainy, with temperatures in the 60s.

If there were one day I wish had been short, it would have been this day's ride.

I wanted to spend as much time with family and friends, so that meant an early start. I was on the road by 5:45 a.m. At 105 miles, I knew it would be a long day. My family would be in Menasha at approximately 1:00, so I didn't take too many breaks.

I had quite a plan that I was trying to pull off, too. After Menasha, my oldest sister, Jan, would take me to Green Bay to attend a wedding. That night we would stay in a motel. The next morning she would take me back down to Menasha where I would ride with the group over to Manitowoc. There, my third sister, Lara, would be waiting for me to take me back to Green Bay. The other riders would take the ferry across Lake Michigan to lower Michigan, where they would spend the next day off. After spending the day and next morning with my sister and her family in Green Bay, they would take me back down to Manitowoc to catch the ferry to join the other riders. I spent my day off in Wisconsin instead of lower Michigan. Wow!

Halfway through the day, I passed a road named "Saddle Sore Lane." Saddle sores are giant boils in the crotch area, and can be a major problem for riders. I had three or four good-sized sores in my crotch that seemed to be festering more by the day. Each morning it seemed like I was sitting on a rock, until the area became numb.

Often times, saddle sores occur because of friction from the saddle or from a wet chamois (the pad in your bike shorts). It's very important to wash your bike shorts daily, and to make sure your saddle is the right height. Though they eventually went away, I've since had one dime-sized saddle sore lanced open.

With about 20 miles to go, I encountered a nasty, three-mile patch of gravel. About halfway through it, a pick-up truck approached me from behind. He stopped and asked if I wanted a ride across. I told him thanks, but no thanks. I think he actually shook his head at me in disbelief…if he only knew.

When I finally made it to Menasha, I experienced a lot of joy. My family soon arrived and the party began! I couldn't believe all the food they brought! My mom almost cried when she saw me because she thought I wasn't eating enough. As other riders began streaming in, they all came over to introduce themselves and eat. I know they all appreciated it and we had a great time. My friend Tom also did an interview with me and took a picture for the paper.

For the first time today, I heard another rider tell me he wished the whole trip were over. I think he missed his family, and was getting tired of riding his bike.

Soon everyone was gone and I was heading for Green Bay. The wedding reception was another reunion for me. A lot of people there had been following me in the paper. One of my good friends who hadn't seen me in a while asked me if I had Leukemia because I was so thin! I got a good laugh out of that one. I don't think I shut my mouth once the entire night. I finally got to bed about 11:30 p.m.

<u>Lake Michigan</u>

Date: July 29, day 42
Start: Menasha, WI
End: Manitowoc, WI
Riding time: 3:15
Miles: 62
Maximum speed: 40 mph
Average speed: 19 mph
Elevation gain: 1,750 feet
Weather: Cloudy, cool, and rainy, with temperatures in the 60s.

I could have slept forever this morning.

All the excitement of the last few days had caught up with me. When my sister took me down to Menasha, most of the group was already gone. I rode alone for a few minutes, but quickly caught up with everyone when we stopped for breakfast.

I ended up riding with a tandem. A tandem is a bike built for two, and is a lot like an 18-wheeler. With the extra weight, it has a hard time going up hill, but when the terrain is flat or downhill, it's extremely fast. Two good cyclists can turn a tandem into a "flying machine." I was able to get a free ride to Manitowoc by staying in their slipstream.

The route was once again pretty insignificant. I knew my sister Lara and nephew would be waiting for me upon finishing, so I wanted to get done early. That was half the reason I rode with the tandem today.

My sister and nephew were waiting for me in Manitowoc when I got there. My nephew Stevie was a big hit with the other riders. Since our lunch spot was about a mile from the ferry, I told my sister that I *had* to ride the last mile down there on my bike. I almost overlooked this small detail in the excitement of the day. I was sure that the next morning when my brother-in-law brought me down to catch the ferry, he would bring me right to the unloading area. That would mean I wouldn't have ridden the last mile from the lunch spot to the boat. I know it's a small detail, but it would have bugged me if I hadn't ridden it.

Manitowoc was once home to strong tribes of Native American Indians. It was their language that gave the city its name. The Indians spoke of "Munedoo-owk" meaning "Home of the Good Spirit."

The shipbuilding industry played a major role in the growth of Manitowoc. Submarines and tankers became the focus of Manitowoc's shipbuilding industry during our country's times of war.

After spending the rest of the afternoon and next morning with my family, my brother-in-law took me back down to Manitowoc to the ferry. Two other Cycle America riders chose to do the same thing I did, so it was nice to have some company.

This seemed like the beginning of the end for me. I became really depressed. I had just spent the last five days with people I knew, and now I was leaving again. I only had three weeks and 1,500 miles to go, but it was very hard to leave.

My bike and I boarded the S.S Badger around noon and began the 60-mile, four-hour journey. The Badger offers an alternate route for passengers who want to travel to lower Michigan, but don't want to drive through Chicago and add distance. The ferry ride not only saves on time and distance, but it's a beautiful trip. If you were to drive from Manitowoc to Ludington, Michigan (where the ferry boat docks), via Chicago, it would be over 400 miles. The one-way fare for a person and a car is $90.

Lake Michigan is the third largest of the five Great Lakes, after Superior and Huron.

About a half hour from Ludington, it began to rain. After the ferryboat ride was completed, I had to ride ten more miles to Scottville, Michigan, on busy Highway 10. I put a white garbage bag over my backpack and me to avoid getting too wet.

"Thundering Falls Spectacular"
Michigan/Ontario

<u>A Long Few Days</u>

Date: July 31, day 44
Start: Scottville, MI
End: Farwell, MI
Riding time: 4:45
Miles: 86
Maximum speed: 28 mph
Average speed: 18.1 mph
Elevation gain: 2,430 feet
Weather: Mostly cloudy and cooler, with temperatures in the 70s.

This was the start of a long few days for me. I am originally from the U.P. of Michigan, but by the end of the week I couldn't wait to get out of the state.

People who live in the U.P. are sometimes called "Yoopers." The name became famous because of a band called The Yoopers. Their biggest hit songs are "Rusty Chevrolet" and "The Second Week of Deer Camp." A movie, "Escanaba in Da Moonlight," is about Yoopers.

The U.P. is a special place to live. It truly is God's country, with a lot of hardwood forests, country back roads, and prime deer hunting. It's also the butt of a lot of cruel jokes, especially from the "Trolls," the residents who live in lower Michigan (because they live below the Mackinac Bridge). I've been asked many times if we have electricity in the U.P. I was once asked if we ever heard of the game Monopoly. I think it's really funny, but a lot of Yoopers take offense to it. I think the Trolls are just jealous of our area.

Since completing Coast-to-Coast 2000, I've gotten a chance to tour the U.P. on bike, and I'd put its scenery up against any in the country.

Yoopers also have a different accent, similar to French Canadians. My favorite bumper sticker from the U.P. says, "Say Yeah to da U.P. Hey!"

The busy highways were also back today. Unlike the U.P., lower Michigan doesn't have as many back roads for bike travel, so we had to ride on a major road, Highway 10. It had been quite some time since I had been on a busy highway, so it took a little while to get used to it again. I really didn't notice how busy it was until I stopped to make a phone call, and saw all the cars whizzing by. It actually made me sort of nervous. It was also very bumpy. When a road is full of traffic and bumpy, it makes for a long day. Instead of concentrating on the scenery, all of your thoughts are directed to the road and your safety.

At mile 44, I passed through Reed City, Michigan, and took a picture of the water tower. Yoopers will remember Reed City because their Coyotes were the victims of the U.P's Stephenson Eagles, the 1981 Michigan Class C Basketball State Champions. The game was especially exciting because one of Stephenson's players hit a 25-footer as time expired in regulation to send the game into overtime. We ended up winning the game, and the state title, too. I went to Stephenson High School (as did all my sisters) and graduated in 1990, so I remember that 1981-year quite well. It reminds me a lot of the movie "Hoosiers," about an Indiana basketball team. The Trolls didn't think that a bunch of hicks from the U.P. could beat them, so the victory was sweet.

Frankenmuth, Michigan

Date: August 1, day 45
Start: Farwell, MI
End: Frankenmuth, MI
Riding time: 5:00
Miles: 93
Maximum speed: 24 mph
Average speed: 18.6 mph
Elevation gain: 810 feet
Weather: Sunny, hot, and humid, with temperatures in the 80s.

You can guess what type of day it was with only 810 feet of elevation gain…a very flat one. This was the flattest day of the summer.

I felt like I had no energy today. Every once in a while, a rider goes through this. The key is being able to snap out of it in time to regain your strength. It wasn't so important to me, but if you're a Tour de France rider, one bad day could cost you the race. Not every day is great for Lance Armstrong, but when he's having a tough ride, he counts on his teammates to give him the support he needs.

I was able to see some Amish farms this day. The Amish are a group of conservative Christian people who believe in simplicity. The Amish immigrated to North America in the early 18th century. They are known for their plain clothing and old-fashioned lifestyle.

I almost took a major spill as well. I was racing down a small hill and failed to negotiate a sharp right-hand turn at the bottom. I didn't realize I was supposed to turn right, and there was some loose gravel at the intersection. I knew I was going too fast to make the turn, but I tried anyway. About halfway into the corner, I felt my back tire slide as I applied the brakes. I made a mad dash for the side of the road, and I managed to pull myself through it while riding in the ditch. I was actually quite proud of myself for not crashing.

If you know you can't make a turn, don't attempt to do it. It's better to go by it, slow to a stop, and turn around. You *never* want to apply your brakes while in a corner (like I did). You should brake *before* you enter it to avoid what almost happened to me. I got lucky, but it could have ended my trip.

Our lunch spot was on Lake Huron, our second Great Lake in three days. Lake Huron is the second largest Great Lake.

Just like Leavenworth, Washington, Frankenmuth, Michigan, is a Bavarian town, but the two have much different histories. If you recall, Leavenworth switched to a Bavarian theme to avoid bankruptcy, but Frankenmuth's roots go directly back to Germany.

Frankenmuth was founded by a group of German-Lutheran missionaries who came to the area to teach Christianity to the Indians. Franken is the province from which the settlers came and Muth means courage in German.

Today, Frankenmuth takes a lot of pride in preserving the German heritage. Area homes, businesses and surrounding farms remain very neat and clean, reflecting the German lifestyle. Flowers and greenery are prevalent and many people consider Frankenmuth the most authentic Bavarian town to be found in the United States.

Frankenmuth is also famous for its food. Two of the country's largest ethnic family restaurants are found in the downtown area.

<u>More Rain</u>

Date: August 2, day 46
Start: Frankenmuth, MI
End: Richmond, MI
Riding time: 4:50
Miles: 92
Maximum speed: 28 mph
Average speed: 19 mph
Elevation gain: 1,420 feet
Weather: Cloudy, cool, and rainy, with temperatures in the 60s.

What a yucky day!

This was the most rain the group encountered during the trip. I actually had to wait after breakfast for over an hour while a thunderstorm came ripping through the area. When the lightning and rain finally let up, I took off. This day reminded me somewhat of the day in South Dakota two weeks before, but without the headwind.

A couple of riders got into a scuffle at breakfast. It all started when one of them parked his recumbent bicycle in a handicap parking spot. The other rider, who happens to have a handicapped brother, took offense at this and asked him to move it. When it wasn't done in a timely manner, their disagreement almost came to blows, but fortunately, cooler heads prevailed.

I got along with everyone on the trip, but I can understand how it wasn't as easy for some people. We'd been with each other for seven weeks now, and people were starting to feel the effects of the trip. I think that was another positive about riding alone; I didn't spend too much time with any one person.

I had a pretty close-knit group of people I spent time with, but all the riders hold a special place in my heart. The riders and their stories make a trip memorable. It was a fascinating group from a statistical standpoint.

Twenty-four states were represented, as was England. Out of the 52 riders, there were 34 men and 18 women. Our oldest rider was 71. The youngest rider was 18.

The majority of riders were married and had families. I was a bit surprised at this, because I don't think I could ever leave a wife and family behind. If you have a companion with similar interests, this trip would be a wonderful opportunity to spend time together. Despite this, only three couples attended together.

I think I was in the ideal situation. I wasn't married and didn't have a girlfriend. I had no family to watch out for, had my summer off, and had responsible people watching my house.

Even though I don't like to talk about individual riders, everyone would agree that there was one very amazing person on the trip, and what he did was simply remarkable. Mark Oncale, the oldest rider, was one of the best. He always rode alone and was among the first to finish. Most people at 71 years old don't think about riding a bicycle 80 miles a day.

A retired crab fisherman from Louisiana, Mark knew what it was like to work hard, and that work ethic helped him make it through the trip. He began riding his bike shortly after his wife died, and like me, his hobby soon turned into much more. The man was in incredible shape and took pride in his body. He would often tell people that he was proof that life could begin after 70.

I remember him talking to my parents in Menasha, and he told them that before he left on the trip, his pastor from Louisiana told him not to forget God. When my dad asked him about it, Mark responded, "When I was riding over those mountains, I remembered God. I said to him, 'Lord help me get over these mountains'." Mark was a hero to all of us. I look at what I did, and I think it was quite an accomplishment; but when I look at what he did, it puts me to shame. He would eventually make it all the way to the Atlantic…riding every mile. Mark is a person who has talent and has learned to use the whole of it. I recently learned that Mark went coast-to-coast again in the summer of 2002, at the age of 73!

Michigan, nicknamed the Wolverine State, became a state in 1837. Ironically, there has never been a sighting of a wolverine in the state. It's an animal similar to a weasel, but only found in the high latitudes. One has to wonder how the nickname came about.

Michigan's name came about from an Indian word meaning "large lake." It's the only one of the 49 continental states to be split into two large land segments, the Upper Peninsula and Lower Peninsula. The Mackinac Bridge, a five-mile-long suspension bridge, connects the two.

I pretty much got "spit on" with rain the rest of the day. There were times it rained so hard, that it actually hurt. There is nothing more uncomfortable than riding in the rain, because you can never, ever get warm. Your jersey becomes like a second skin. Rain drenches it, cementing it to your body, so the coldness mingles with your sweat and seeps into your bones. Your muscles seize up and grow heavy with exhaustion. I would much rather start a ride and then have it start raining, but I was wet from the start. I have a picture of me sitting on a curb after finishing the day into Richmond, and I have mud caked all over my face and legs.

This day was really flat, and there is nothing more demoralizing than a long flat road in the rain. At least on a climb, your body stays a little bit warm because you have to work so hard, but on a flat road, you just get cold and wet to the bone. No bootie or jacket is good enough.

Richmond really wasn't one my favorite overnight towns. You can really get a feel for a town when riding into it, and Richmond had a ton of road construction, and not much to see. Maybe I was just in a bad mood from the long distance and constant rain.

<u>Canada!</u>

Date: August 3, day 47
Start: Richmond, MI
End: West Lorne, Ontario, Canada
Riding time: 4:00
Miles: 78
Maximum speed: 30 mph
Average speed: 19.5 mph
Elevation gain: 1,000 feet
Weather: Mostly sunny and warm, with temperatures in the 70s.

I was sure glad to get out of Michigan and enter foreign soil.

After only 22 miles of riding, I entered Marine City, Michigan, and the customs area. I would have to take another ferryboat (the second of the trip so far) across the St. Claire River into Ontario, Canada. When I got there, I was the only rider, but soon five or six others showed up. The ferry ride only took about five minutes.

The night before, Greg Walsh had told us to make sure we had some form of identification to show at the border. I guess I was expecting a long, drawn-out process, but it went smoothly. When I've gone to Canada in the past, the custom agents usually asked quite a few questions about where we were going and what our plans were. All the agents asked us on this day was if we were from Cycle America. Since we said yes, we were able to go right through. I guess it pays to be on a coast-to-coast bicycle tour!

I was amazed at how clean the roads were in Canada. I don't remember seeing one piece of garbage the entire day. From what I saw, Canadians take a lot of pride in their country.

It was also different seeing the speed limit signs in kilometers per hour instead of miles per hour. Most U.S. citizens are so used to the English system they have no idea about how to convert. I'm pretty sure the United States is one of the only industrialized countries in the world that doesn't use the metric system. If you're wondering, one mile equals .623 kilometers.

Many Canadians speak French, but I don't remember seeing too many signs that weren't in English. With its close proximity to the U.S., Ontario residents live a lot like U.S. citizens, but they just happen to live in another country.

Ontario is Canada's second largest province, and stretches for almost 1,000 miles in length and width. Ontario borders four of the five Great Lakes. The only one it doesn't touch is Michigan. Ontario is primarily an agricultural region. On only ten percent of its land, half of the nation's agricultural and manufactured goods are produced! Also, one-third of Canada's entire population lives in Ontario.

<u>Lake Erie</u>

Date: August 4, day 48
Start: West Lorne, Ontario, Canada
End: Port Dover, Ontario, Canada
Riding time: 5:30
Miles: 101
Maximum speed: 40 mph
Average speed: 18.4 mph
Elevation gain: 2,200 feet
Weather: Sunny and warm, with temperatures in the 70s.

One hundred miles…plus one!

This was the fifth time in my life I rode 100 miles on a bike in a single day (I've since done it several times more). I've probably done another dozen rides of 90 or more, but I suppose ten miles doesn't mean a whole lot. Any time the mileage was close to 100 for the day (but not over), I had ambitions to ride the few extra miles to make it an even 100, but not once did that happen on the trip. I guess by the end of the day, five extra miles was the last thing on my mind.

I've done plenty of rides in the past that I would consider "centuries," even though the mileage didn't add up to 100. That cold, rainy day in South Dakota was only 95 miles, but it was the longest number of hours I've spent on my bike. It all depends on the terrain and weather conditions.

When training, a cyclist has to keep in mind that time and intensity on the bike are much more important than distance. Too many cyclists get caught up in how far they've gone, instead of evaluating the ride as a whole. It's a good idea to tell yourself before each ride what your goal is.

I break up my training into three different categories: The first is what I call exercise. Exercise is going out for a quick spin on the bike, walking, or doing any other activity that really doesn't get the heart rate up too high. It does serve a purpose, but when I exercise, I know I'm not really gaining any fitness. It may also follow a really tough ride day, so it lets my body recover. I call the next stage working out. It's a slightly higher intensity than exercise, but still is pretty low. Most of my riding is done in this mode. The final type for me is training. This is a high intensity for an extended period of time. I only train a couple of times a week at most, because it's such a stress on the body. If you do too many days of high intensity workouts in a row, your body will feel the effects and start to shut down.

It's important to rest as hard as you train, but when I say rest, I don't mean sitting on the couch eating chips and drinking soda. Rest is rest from the bike, not rest from training.

To find your maximum heart rate (which is genetically determined) you need to conduct a simple test. By using a heart monitor (a device that straps around your chest and emits a signal to a wristwatch that you wear) it's pretty easy to find. After a good warm-up on your bike, do an all-out burst for a couple of minutes to see what your maximum was. If you don't have access to a monitor, you can use the formula 220 minus your age as a gauge. It's not completely accurate, but it will give you a general idea of what it is. You could also go to a cardiologist to have it checked out.

Your maximum heart rate will decrease with age, so 160 beats per minute (BPM) in a 20-year old is much different than in a 50-year old. For example: A 50-year-old's maximum heart rate is probably around 170, while a 20-year-old's maximum is closer to 200. If these two riders each get their heart rates up to 160, the older rider will be close to his maximum, and will not be able to continue at such a pace for very long; while the younger rider still has plenty of room to raise his heart rate, closer to his maximum.

Lance Armstrong actually has a lower maximum heart rate than other riders. Compared to his teammate George Hincapie, it's 20 beats lower.

On easy riding days, you want to keep your heart rate between 60 – 70 percent of its maximum. Using a 20 year-old person as an example, that would mean keeping it between 120 and 140 BPM. When trying to gain aerobic fitness, you should strive for 70 – 80 percent, or 140 – 160 BPM. To see substantial gains in your fitness, you need to ride at a higher intensity, say 80 – 90 percent of your maximum heart rate. This means keeping your heart rate between 160 and 180 BPM.

To gain speed on your bike, you need to ride harder and faster. To gain endurance, your training speed should be slower, but for a longer duration.

More importantly, as your fitness level increases, the better your body becomes at removing oxygen from circulating blood, and then converting it into usable energy by your body tissues. This is called VO2 max. VO2 max is the maximum amount of oxygen in milliliters, one can use in one minute per kilogram of body weight. Those who are more fit have higher VO2 max values and can exercise more intensely than those who are not as well conditioned. Numerous studies show that your VO2 max is genetically determined, but you can increase it slightly by working out at an intensity that raises your heart rate to between 65 and 85 percent of its maximum.

Most elite athletes have VO2 max values in the 60s or 70s, but Lance Armstrong's is normally 84! This means that Lance's body can use 84 milliliters of oxygen every minute, for every kilogram he weighs. Lance weighs about 75 kilos, so his body uses about 6,300 milliliters of oxygen per minute! The average 30-year-old American male can expect to have a VO2 max in the 30s or 40s.

It's important to realize that giving your body more oxygen will not improve its ability to perform at a higher level; it's how well your body is able to use the oxygen it has (VO2 max). Therefore, when you see football players (or other athletes) huffing on oxygen during a game, it doesn't serve a real purpose. These athletes need to increase their fitness, so their body becomes better equipped to use the oxygen it has.

It's also been shown that muscle fibers are either slow twitch or fast twitch. If you're a sprinter, you probably have more fast twitch fibers (which can produce faster speeds). If endurance is your forte, you more than likely have slow twitch fibers in your legs (which don't fatigue as fast, but can't produce explosive speeds). It's possible to gain either type of muscle fiber by riding a specific way.

My Great Lakes tour continued today with Lake Erie, our third Great Lake in seven days. Lake Erie is fourth in size, with a surface area of 9,900 square miles. Pollution of the lake in the 1960s caused many beaches and resorts to close, but by the late 1970s, environmental damage was on the decline.

I got a chance to view the lake up close in Port Stanley, Ontario. I took an alternate route so I was able to get above the lake. It was a very pretty sight. The worst part about seeing it was the massive climb I had to do to get there.

After leaving the scenic vantage point, I rode into town and visited the beach. I never realized it before, but a lot of cities groom the sand to make it look perfect for swimmers and tourists who plan a day there. I saw a machine that was rolling the sand to smooth it out.

With the long mileage, I also decided to ride with a group today. We played a lot of games, often sprinting for road signs and going hard on climbs.

Sprinting can be very dangerous, especially at the pro level. It can be a battle royal, as a lot of elbows and arms are being flung around. You'll seldom see Lance Armstrong contesting a sprint in the Tour de France, because it's too dangerous. He realizes that his Tour could end with one wrong move, and the worst place he could be is at the front of the pack during a sprint finish. Speeds during a sprint finish often exceed 40 mph.

I found out how dangerous sprinting is during a race in the summer of 2002. The race started off innocently enough, but didn't stay that way for long, as the speed quickly jumped to a mind-boggling 30 mph (we averaged 26 for the whole race). The terrain was demanding, but not difficult enough to break up the big field, so by the end there were still 60 "testosterone-drenched" men trying to win (myself included). The last thing I remember was lying in the ditch looking up at the sky wondering what the heck had happened (I still have no idea). I crashed at almost 40 mph and cracked my helmet in four places. I also received plenty of road rash on my hip, butt, and back. My buddy ended up taking me to the hospital where I was diagnosed with a mild concussion, but no other serious injuries. The doctor figured I was probably unconscious for about 20 seconds, and knocked out when my head hit the pavement. (I'm glad I don't remember anything about the crash.) I guess in retrospect I shouldn't have been contesting a sprint of that nature, but I am very competitive. It didn't affect me too much, though, because the next week I was bumping elbows and racing again, managing to get a top-ten finish.

If there's anything positive that's come about from the whole ordeal, it's made me realize the importance of wearing a crash helmet. I still have that cracked helmet, and every time I look at it, I realize that it probably saved my life.

Sprinters are fascinating athletes. They suffer so much during a race to get over the climbs and to the finish; but in the final few miles, they are transformed and reborn to do astonishing things. Where they get the power to sprint at speeds of 40 mph after riding 150 miles is beyond belief.

The first overnight in Canada was Port Dover, Ontario, which is situated on the North Shore of Lake Erie. This port city is the home of the world's largest fresh water fishing fleet. The city beach is a big tourist attraction as well, so swimming is popular in the area. Because of its shallow depth, the port is the site of numerous shipwrecks.

<u>Niagara Falls</u>

Date: August 5, day 49
Start: Port Dover, Ontario, Canada
End: Niagara Falls, Ontario, Canada
Riding time: 3:45
Miles: 70
Maximum speed: 31 mph
Average speed: 18.7 mph
Elevation gain: 1,130 feet
Weather: Sunny and hot, with temperatures in the 80s.

I had seen Niagara Falls only once in the past, so I was excited to get done early today. Heaven forbid that I ever do this someday, but one of my sisters and her husband took me there on their honeymoon!

Before arriving at the falls, I cycled with a man from the area with whom I had quite an interesting conversation. I commented to him on how courteous the area drivers were to me. He told me it was probably because a former pro cyclist, Steve Bauer, came from the area. Bauer won the bronze medal in the 1988 Olympic Road Race, and also took second place in the 1990 Paris-Roubaix (by less than an inch). He went on to have a very successful pro career, and just recently retired.

Shortly after lunch, I took my third ferryboat ride of the trip across the Welland Canal. There used to be a bridge here, but 25 years ago, an out of control barge slammed into it, knocking it into the river. Instead of paying millions of dollars to replace it, the company that insured the bridge thought it was better to hire a man to run a ferry service to shuttle people and bikes across the canal. They figured a year's salary, plus upkeep of the equipment was a lot cheaper than building a bridge, when motorists can go five or six miles up the road and cross over the canal on another bridge.

Niagara Falls, one of the world's most spectacular natural wonders, is known for its beauty, famous attractions, and daredevil stunts.

The falls are located on the Niagara River. The Niagara flows 35 miles from Lake Erie to Lake Ontario. They were first explored by French missionaries, and during the War of 1812, the British and Americans fought over them.

Over the years, the hard rock and limestone have eroded, pushing the falls back toward Lake Erie. Until the 1950s, erosion caused the falls to recede three feet per year, but thanks to less water flow, that rate has dropped to less than one foot per year.

Niagara Falls is actually made up of two separate falls, Horseshoe Falls on the Canadian side, and American Falls on the U.S. side. Ninety percent of the water in the Niagara River goes over Horseshoe Falls, which is 170 feet tall (comparable to a 16-story building). The other ten percent flows over American Falls, 184 feet high. In all, about 50 million gallons of water goes over these two falls every minute!

Bob Goldberg (along with Floyd's wife, Beth) also decided that part of Floyd's remaining ashes would be thrown over the falls. In a small ceremony, Bob put some of Floyd in a small bottle cap, taped it up, and threw it in the Niagara River. He watched as Floyd went "bottle capping" over the falls.

Our second to last day off also occurred at Niagara Falls. I spent the day sightseeing and going to church for the first time while on the trip.

"Empire Strikes Back"
New York

<u>Back in the U.S.</u>

Date: August 7, day 50
Start: Niagara Falls, Ontario, Canada
End: Albion, NY
Riding time: 3:50
Miles: 76
Maximum speed: 40 mph
Average speed: 20 mph
Elevation gain: 1,740 feet
Weather: Mostly sunny and hot, with temperatures in the 80s.

An endless supply of rainbows!

Have you ever had the experience of eating breakfast 350 feet above Niagara Falls? If you haven't, I highly recommend taking a trip up the Minolta Tower to do so. The view is breathtaking, the food is great, and there's even an open-air observatory where you can watch the falls window-free.

After leaving breakfast, I almost took a nasty "digger" descending a hill. There was a light mist falling, and that caused slippery conditions. I was going too fast and had to lock up my back brakes in order to stop for an intersection. My back tire fishtailed, but I managed to stay upright.

A cyclist should be especially cautious when rain begins, particularly if it's been dry for a few days. Oil and dust will float to the road surface, making traction treacherous; but as rain continues and washes this slippery stuff away, traction may become almost as secure as on a dry road. Nevertheless, painted lines and steel surfaces (manhole covers, grates, railroad tracks, expansion joints) are always slick when wet.

The 1993 World Cycling Championship held in Oslo, Norway, took place in the pouring rain, and was a classic example of just how slippery roads can get when wet. There were cyclists falling at every corner. I've never seen a race that had so many crashes. Even though he fell twice, Lance Armstrong showed he had awesome bike-handling skills and went on to win the event, thus becoming the youngest world champion ever.

I crossed over the Rainbow Bridge to the United States. The bridge is named because a rainbow is always visible while crossing. I also saw how little water actually flows over the falls. Authorities have done a lot of work to divert a large portion of the water from the Niagara River elsewhere to combat erosion. I was able to see lots of boulders just upstream from the falls. It really is quite shallow.

Re-entering the United States at the border was no problem. All I had to do was state my citizenship, and I was able to pass right through.

Most of the ride was right along Lake Ontario, on Highway 18; it was very pretty. Highway 18 is perfect for cycling. It has a very wide shoulder and low vehicle traffic.

Lake Ontario is the smallest of the Great Lakes, and also the farthest east. The area of the lake is 7,550 square miles. Lake Ontario completed my Great Lakes tour. I was able to view four of the Great Lakes in an eight-day period. The only one I didn't see on the trip was Superior, and I've seen that plenty of other times.

I also talked to my father when I finished the day's ride, and he informed me that the Bitterroot Valley in Montana was completely engulfed in flames. Firefighters from across the United States and Canada were being sent to the area to try to contain the fire, which had already burned four million acres. It was hard to imagine it burning, as we had passed through it only a few weeks ago.

My resting heart rate this morning was only 36 BPM. Under normal circumstances, a low heart rate is not all that great and can be a sign of a serious problem, but under these circumstances, it was okay. The heart is a muscle, so when it becomes bigger and stronger, it pumps less often, while still supplying the body with the oxygen it needs. If you were to stop exercising over a period of time (maybe a month), you would notice your resting heart rate would increase. A decrease in your resting heart rate is a sign of gained fitness. Conversely, an elevated resting heart rate is a sign that you're over-working your body. If you continue to push your body even though you have an elevated resting heart rate, it will lead to fatigue, weight loss, and decreased performance. I tried to take it every day to see how my body was responding to its punishment. When I started the trip, it was 42.

Five-time Tour de France winner, Miguel Indurain, had a resting heart rate of 28 BPM! During a race, it would rise to 150, but it wouldn't stay there for long. Thirty seconds after ending his race, his heart rate was down to 60 BPM! A quick drop in heart rate after intense exercise is a sign of excellent fitness.

Most professional cyclists don't have resting heart rates that low, but many are in the 30s and 40s.

<u>Erie Canal</u>

Date: August 8, day 52
Start: Albion, NY
End: Sodus, NY
Riding time: 4:30
Miles: 84
Maximum speed: 33 mph
Average speed: 18.7 mph
Elevation gain: 1910 feet
Weather: Sunny and hot, with temperatures in the 80s.

The Erie Canal runs 363 miles, and connects the Great Lakes to New York City via the Hudson River.

The canal proved to be well worth the money, as many settlers from the East began traveling to the Midwest. They were able to ship their farm products back east via the canal, and have supplies for their use shipped to them. Today the canal is primarily used for pleasure boating.

Thirty miles of our biking route was along the canal. Unfortunately, it was rather difficult to view it because my mind was elsewhere. Cycle America wanted us to avoid going through Rochester, New York, so they opted to put us through an obstacle course to get around it. The obstacle course was a bike path with about as many turns as a ferris wheel. It tested my ability to follow a yellow arrow, that's for sure! It was also extremely bumpy and full of debris. It was common to be pedaling along at 20 mph, and suddenly come upon a bump in the path that was big enough to almost throw you from your bike. Cycle America did a ***great*** job, though, routing us around the big city. From what I saw of Rochester, I was glad we didn't go through it.

We also didn't have services on the bike path, so that was a problem. Unlike other bike paths, I was a little uneasy on this one. I saw a lot of graffiti on bridges that I passed and a lot of rundown houses as well.

The coast-to-coast riders had a big meeting on this night. It was very emotional for all of us, and a lot of riders couldn't make it through without crying. I got pretty choked up myself. Each of the riders was given the floor for a few minutes to discuss their thoughts about the summer. For some reason, I was really nervous about speaking. Being a teacher, I'm used to talking in front of large groups, so I wasn't sure why I was nervous. I started by saying I knew beyond a shadow of a doubt, that finishing in Gloucester would be the happiest day of my life so far. I also discussed how the trip would make me a better person and teacher, because I could think back to the hardships I faced this summer, and realize that life (to me) isn't that hard compared to what I did in the summer of 2000.

Perhaps Jersey Joe summed up the summer for all of us. He said that riding our bikes made us happy, and that after working and being around "pissed off" people our whole lives, this summer allowed us to be kids again.

Greg Walsh also tried to prepare us for the end of the ride, by saying how difficult it would be for some of us to return to our normal way of living after the tour. I guess I hadn't thought about it very much, but I could see where it might be a problem, because I hadn't exactly been living normally the last nine weeks.

Jan Clark from Colorado told everyone that if it were up to her, she would turn around and go back across the country when we hit the Atlantic! She simply didn't want the experience to end.

Greg was also the bearer of some bad news for us. He informed the group that Lolo and Lost Trail Pass in Montana were both completely destroyed in the fires, and were closed off to vehicle traffic.

<u>Mexico, New York?</u>

Date: August 9, day 53
Start: Sodus, NY
End: Mexico, NY
Riding time: 3:40
Miles: 73
Maximum speed: 45 mph
Average speed: 20 mph
Elevation gain: 3,130 feet
Weather: Sunny and warm, with temperatures in the 70s.

Mexico, New York, is just east of Sweden, Greece, Ontario, and Egypt. It's a bit to the north of Phoenix, and slightly south of Texas.

Whoever named these towns was really confused.

Mexico is a small community of 1,500 close to Lake Ontario. George Scriba, a land speculator, founded it. Scriba may have used the name "Mexico" because he had heard it when he was in the West Indies before coming to New York.

Mexico grew because it had the best soil and water of any place around. Up until 2001, Mexico's water had not been chlorinated. In 1991, Mexico won the state competition for the best tasting water in the state.

Mexico is also famous for being a town associated with the Underground Railroad, a secret transportation route for runaway slaves traveling to the north. Though neither underground nor a railroad, it was named because its activities had to be carried out in secret, using darkness or disguise, and because railway terms were used in reference to the system. The slaves' ultimate goal was to make it to the promised land of Canada. The bookstore that I visited in town was a known hideout for the Underground Railroad.

The Mexico Academy and Central School (where we stayed) is home to a beautiful mural called "La Guerre d' Independence." The mural depicts the Americans' War of Independence. A gift from France, there are only two in existence, the one in Mexico, and the other one in the White House. Apparently, though, the one in Mexico is in much better condition.

Before arriving in Mexico, I took another detour to Sodus Point, New York, via Highway 14. Sodus Point is a maritime city on the shores of Lake Ontario. I was able to walk to the lighthouse about 100 yards out into the lake. The excursion to Sodus Point added 12 miles onto my ride, but it was well worth it.

Since I like to ride fairly fast, I would usually get to lunch early. There were often times when lunch wasn't even set up when I got there. On this day I was late, and I got some razzing for it. The Sodus Point detour not only added a few bonus miles, but it gave the other riders a reason to pick on me. A few of them even joked that this was the first time they'd seen me in weeks!

A consequence of getting done early was having to unload the "Penske," Cycle America's yellow rental truck that followed us across the country carrying our luggage. When I got done each day, I usually had to wait for the truck along with a couple other riders. When it finally arrived, we would unload all the riders' gear and put it into a nice, neat pile. It only took a few minutes to unload, but it was a difficult job after riding all day. Although I never purposely dawdled to avoid unloading it, my detour also gave me a day off from doing that. I remember one rider being so excited one day because she got done early enough to unload the Penske!

<u>Sackets Harbor</u>

Date: August 10, day 54
Start: Mexico, NY
End: Watertown, NY
Riding time: 3:10
Miles: 60
Maximum speed: 38 mph
Average speed: 19 mph
Elevation gain: 2,200 feet
Weather: Sunny and hot, with temperatures in the 80s.

New York is beautiful!

With the short mileage, I took another detour towards the end of the ride to take in a little history and visit Sackets Harbor, New York. Had it not been for Sackets Harbor, the entire course of American History may have changed.

It was here that a great military and naval operation defended the nation's northern border in the War of 1812 with the British. Were it not for the successful defense of the harbor, this section of the country might actually be a part of Canada today.

Because of its deep water, Sackets was the main U.S. base on Lake Ontario. This extremely critical post saw one of the first engagements of the war.

The British actually defeated ***themselves*** in this battle.

The U.S Militia, which was positioned on the shore, used a 32-pound cannon, but had only 24-pound cannonballs on hand. They were seen wrapping the 24-pounders in carpet, and then shoving them into their 32-pound cannon. Obviously, their projectiles didn't come close to their intended targets. The British made the mistake of shooting a single 24-pounder over, which struck near the U.S.'s cannon. The U.S. gunmen quickly dug it up, loaded it, and shot it out into the harbor. It struck and sunk a British ship, forcing the whole British Navy to retreat! Thank you British!

This was my idea of another awesome day of bicycle touring. There weren't too many times on the trip that the distance was this low, and the scenery this beautiful. Sackets Harbor was absolutely stunning in my eyes.

With the shorter mileage, a cyclist has a chance to do a lot more sightseeing than normal, because they're not worrying about riding 100 miles and getting to the next town.

Leaving Sackets Harbor I heard my own "War of 1812 blast," as I received my eighth flat tire of the trip.

I ended up with ten flats for the entire summer. I don't really think that was an unusually large number considering the condition of some of the roads we traveled. It averaged out to about one a week. One rider from Arizona had 18!

The group stayed in the second city named Watertown. The Watertown in New York is slightly larger than the one in South Dakota. Watertown, New York, lies only ten miles to the east of Lake Ontario, and is famous for getting tons of lake-effect snow in the winter.

<u>Finally a Real Bed!</u>

Date: August 11, day 55
Start: Watertown, NY
End: Star Lake, NY
Riding time: 3:20
Miles: 60
Maximum speed: 32 mph
Average speed: 18 mph
Elevation gain: 2,650 feet
Weather: Cloudy, cool, and rainy, with temperatures in the 60s.

When a lot of people think of New York, they think of big cities and air pollution. However, not all of New York is like that. The upper part is extremely beautiful with rolling terrain and green foliage. It was perhaps the most serene area of the country (except Wisconsin, of course). I once read that New York is in the top two or three in the nation in the production of dairy products.

Much of upstate New York is in Adirondack State Park, the largest state or national park outside of Alaska. The park covers 9,400 square miles, or one-fifth of the state and is about the size of Vermont. Much of it is in a very primitive state, protected by law. The Adirondack Mountains are not like the mountains out West, which are jagged and rough. The Adirondacks are basically "rounded hills." The highest point in the range is Mount Marcy, at 5,344 feet. The name Adirondack is derived from an Iroquois word meaning "eater of tree bark." The French explorer Samuel Champlain first set foot in the Adirondacks in 1609.

Route 3 in New York is an excellent road for cycling. It has very wide shoulders, low traffic, lots of history, and beautiful scenery. There were also a lot of signs on it that told the automobile drivers to share the road with cyclists. Since it's such a popular route for bikers, I think the drivers are more considerate of them. It's nice to know that some states promote fitness and recreation through cycling, and New York is definitely one of them.

My destination was Star Lake, New York, a quaint village in the upper portion of the state. There really wasn't much of a town, but it thrives on the tourist industry. I managed to beat the raindrops again, but others weren't so lucky. They reported getting caught in quite a storm, and many had to wait it out until it passed.

The group stayed at the beautiful Star Lake Campus. It wasn't a college, but more like a camp. There were probably a dozen staff members working there throughout the summer. It was definitely the most luxurious accommodations we had the entire trip. There was a TV, a dining hall, a lake to go swimming in, and bunk beds! After sleeping almost eight weeks on gym floors, I was ready for this. What I wasn't ready for was the snoring. What started out as a quiet evening in the bunkhouse, turned into a night of survival. I sure could have used a pair of earplugs, as "King" Sid was in rare form. Can you imagine sleeping in a bunkhouse with 30 other men? There were all sorts of interesting sounds that night. I've never had to experience that growing up, and I don't think I want to again. I wanted my sisters back!

<u>Lake Placid, New York</u>

Date: August 12, day 56
Start: Star Lake, NY
End: Lake Placid, NY
Riding time: 4:00
Miles: 74
Maximum speed: 40 mph
Average speed: 18.5 mph
Elevation gain: 3,670 feet
Weather: Mostly cloudy and warm, with temperatures in the 70s.

This was a great day!

Not only was it my birthday, I also got to view some great American history in Lake Placid, New York, home of the 1932 and 1980 Winter Olympics. The only negative was getting a flat tire, but that happened before the ride even started.

We encountered the first hills since leaving Canada. There were a lot of "rollers" on this day's route. There really wasn't a whole lot of flat terrain; you were either going up or down.

I was wondering if anyone would remember my birthday, as I was turning 28. At breakfast, someone caught wind of it, so the group sang "Happy Birthday" to me. When I got to the lunch spot, Cycle America had made a cake for me, too. They were always really good about doing that sort of thing. It's tough to be away from home on your birthday, so it was very nice of them to remember me. My family also sent me a care package full of goodies. I got a cheese hat (a hat made of fake cheese), a new bike jersey, and a bunch of candy.

"Wisconsinites" are often referred to as "cheese heads" because of the amount of cheese they make and consume.

Entering Lake Placid, I stopped at a lacrosse tournament. Lacrosse is a fast and physical sport played out East, but hasn't really caught on in too many other parts of the country. Ten players to a side use long handled racket-like sticks (crosses) to catch, throw, or carry a ball down the field or into the opponents' goal.

The Indians used to play lacrosse, and it was actually much rougher than it is today. As many as a 1,000 players would take part on each side, as goals were often miles apart, and games could take up to three days to complete. Players would disable as many opponents as possible with their stick, and then concentrate on scoring a goal. It was considered excellent training for combat.

According to one of the spectators I talked to, some of the best players from the United States and Canada were in Lake Placid over the weekend for the tournament.

Lake Placid is one of only three cities in the world to have hosted more than one Winter Olympics. I was able to tour many of the Olympic facilities on our last day off. My first stop was the 1932 Olympic ice arena. After that, I walked the short distance over to the newer modern arena. It was here that the United States beat Russia in ice hockey in the 1980 Olympics, and went on to beat Finland in the finals to capture the gold medal. I'm guessing if you asked 1,000 people about the best Olympic moment in United States history, 999 would say this game. I got goose bumps while in the arena.

From there I walked over to Lake Placid High School, and the Olympic speed skating rink, which encircles the school. More history was made here, as Eric Heiden was the first Olympic speed skater to win all five speed-skating events in the same Olympics. He set Olympic records in all five events as well.

During the Olympics, the high school was turned into the press headquarters for the media and photographers. The superintendent of schools had written into the contract a clause allowing him to sit on the roof of the school and watch the speed-skating events. Lake Placid High School is also the only school in the United States to ever be issued a liquor license. It was given one for two weeks during the Olympics so the press could have their beer and wine!

My last stop was the Olympic ski-jumping complex. Soon I was on my way to the top via elevator, and 500 feet off the ground. Since the elevator had glass windows, I spent more time looking at the floor than I did out the windows. This was probably the highest my heart rate got on the whole trip! Another rider asked me if I would ride my bike off the ski jump for a million dollars, and I said, "Nope!"

After reaching the top, I could see for miles on end, witnessing the highest peaks in the Adirondacks; it was definitely very beautiful.

The rest of my day was spent watching the lacrosse tournament.

"History Maker"
New England

<u>Vermont</u>

Date: August 14, day 58
Start: Lake Placid, NY
End: Burlington, VT
Riding time: 2:30
Miles: 50
Maximum speed: 42 mph
Average speed: 20 mph
Elevation gain: 2,300 feet
Weather: Mostly cloudy and warm, with temperatures in the 70s.

The highlight of this day was taking our last ferryboat ride of the trip across Lake Champlain.

Lake Champlain is the border between Vermont and New York, and has an area of 435 square miles. French explorer Samuel D. Champlain, for whom it is named, first visited the lake. It was also the site of many battles of the Revolutionary and the War of 1812.

The hour-long ferryboat ride took me to Burlington, Vermont, and my eleventh state or province. Burlington is home to the University of Vermont and is the largest city in the state. If you're ever in Burlington, be sure to check out the downtown area because it's closed off to vehicle traffic and full of many interesting sights.

Burlington is surrounded by the Green Mountains. The Green Mountains are a part of the Appalachian chain that transverses much of Vermont.

Earlier in the day I had hoped to climb up Whiteface Mountain, the home of the 1980 Olympic skiing events, but I had a flat tire right before I got there, so I decided against it. Bikes are not allowed all the way up the climb, but I could have gone at least halfway up.

With nothing else to do, I shaved my legs today. A lot of cyclists shave their legs to avoid infection from road rash (a rash you get when you crash and your skin rubs on the road). Road rash heals much quicker when there isn't hair in the wound. Others do it so massage is easier. Unlike swimmers (who also shave their body), cyclists don't get much of an aerodynamic advantage from shaving.

Sometimes I get a lot of flack from people for doing it, but it's far better than the alternative…an infection.

As I said earlier, I initially signed up for Coast-to-Coast 2000 for the physical challenge, but a number of riders did so to raise money for various charities. I'm sure well over $100,000 was raised. As far as I know, Bob Hunt from New York raised the most, at over $25,000! He was riding for the Rotary Foundation, so therefore (you guessed it), he became known among the riders as "Rotary Bob."

<u>Ice Cream!</u>

Date: August 15, day 59
Start: Burlington, VT
End: Stowe, VT
Riding time: 4:15
Miles: 75
Maximum speed: 46 mph
Average speed: 17.6 mph
Elevation gain: 5,230 feet
Weather: Mostly sunny and warm, with temperatures in the 70s.

Since I hadn't really done a lot of climbing lately, I took in an additional 25 miles to climb Smuggler's Notch…BIG mistake. I knew that the climbs out East were steeper, but this one was extreme.

Smuggler's Notch is about 12 miles northwest of Stowe, Vermont, on Highway 108. It's a gap between Mount Mansfield, the highest point in Vermont, and Sterling Peak. The roadway is so isolated, that in the winter, the gap narrows enough to be closed to vehicle traffic. People on snowshoes, skiers, and other hikers are the only ones able to access it when the snow flies. The rocks on the Notch are 400 million years old. It was made famous because smugglers used the route, therefore the name. The Embargo Act, which made trade illegal with Canada and Great Britain, also made the route popular with Vermonters. Later on, fleeing slaves escaped through the Notch, and during Prohibition in the 1920s, liquor was brought in from Canada on the improved road.

The climb itself started out innocently enough, but that quickly changed. The bottom portion was a normal gradient, but about a mile from the top, it tipped skyward. It was definitely the steepest climb I've ever done in my life. The road was very windy and narrow, so I was in my lowest gear and barely able to turn the pedals over. I almost fell over on a few occasions. I managed to make it to the top without stopping, so I was happy with myself. The road was only wide enough for one car, so I don't know what happens when a car from each direction tries to use the road. Going down was just as scary. I had to ride my brakes for a good portion so I didn't plummet off the side of the road.

At mile 40 I was able to tour the Ben and Jerry's Ice Cream Factory. Ben and Jerry's has a rags-to-riches story that goes along with it.

The two men took a correspondence course from Penn State University on how to make ice cream. At first they did everything by hand, but soon bought an old gas station and turned it into an ice cream shop. Eventually, they became well known enough in the Burlington and Stowe area that they built a larger plant.

Stowe is also famous because it's where the Von Trapp family settled after fleeing Austria. The Trapp singers began singing in the 1930s, and eventually fled Austria and settled in the region around Stowe in the 1940s. The Trapp's story is told in "The Sound of Music," one of the most successful musicals in theatre history.

Stowe is an absolutely beautiful town. It had plenty of history, tourist attractions, and beautiful scenery. It was one of my favorite towns on the trip.

Traveling the U.S. on a bicycle lets you experience things first-hand, and one thing I really noticed was how the demeanor of the people changed as I got farther east. There were times that I would say hi to someone, and they wouldn't respond to me. It seemed like they were too busy with their own life to even notice me. I thought the people in the West and Midwest were more polite and hospitable.

<u>New Hampshire</u>

Date: August 16, day 60
Start: Stowe, VT
End: Littleton, NH
Riding time: 4:20
Miles: 77
Maximum speed: 48 mph
Average speed: 17.8 mph
Elevation gain: 5,050 feet
Weather: Cloudy, warm, and rainy, with temperatures in the 70s.

I woke up in a puddle of water this morning.

I had a nice funeral for my tent as I tossed it in the garbage. It had so many holes in it that I could actually see the rain dripping through. I didn't really care how I would spend the remaining few days of the trip, but I was pretty sure there were inside arrangements for the duration. I had a few good buddies who I'm sure would have let me stay in their tent, had I needed to.

Shortly after starting, I passed the only covered railroad bridge in Vermont still in operation. The Fisher Railroad Bridge is a 103-foot long bridge built across the Lamoille River. It has a full-length cupola (a structure built on the top of a roof), which served to vent smoke and steam from passing locomotives.

If you're ever in the area, a must-see is South Peachman, Vermont. Our route manager told us that South Peachman is one of the most photographed villages in Vermont. It was settled in 1776 and is very pretty.

Usually, going from state to state did not include going over a river, but entering into New Hampshire did. The Connecticut River is the longest river in New England. The river starts in New Hampshire and then becomes the border between Vermont and New Hampshire. It's one of the most developed rivers in the country in terms of hydro-electric power.

The name Connecticut comes from the Indian word meaning "the long river."

Once while in Wyoming, I slept outside and saw the Northern Lights. I wouldn't see them again until Littleton, New Hampshire.

The Northern Lights are an illumination of the atmosphere that occurs in the higher latitudes in North America. The Northern Lights take many forms, including luminous arcs, bands, and patches. Many times they appear green or red, but eventually fade to a white color. The Northern Lights almost appear to be rippled drapery. I've seen them plenty of times in Wisconsin.

Littleton was founded in 1770, but it wasn't until after the Revolutionary War ended, that the town began to thrive. Today, Littleton is known as a tourist area and for its breathtaking scenery.

<u>Maine</u>

Date: August 17, day 61
Start: Littleton, NH
End: Fryeburg, ME
Riding time: 4:20
Miles: 80
Maximum speed: 56 mph
Average speed: 18.5 mph
Elevation gain: 5,090 feet
Weather: Cloudy and cooler, with temperatures ranging from 48
        to 70 degrees.

I was able to cycle on the Kancamagus Highway today.

It's perhaps one of the most beautiful roads in the East, but it's also extremely hilly. Kancamagus was an Indian chief among the Algonquian Indians in the early 1700s.

The climb itself was about ten miles and came in two separate parts. Although the top of the pass was only 2,860 feet high, it was pretty steep. It had been a while since I'd climbed an actual pass, so it was a good feeling to do it again. At 48 degrees, it was also cold at the top. I remember sitting at the Kancamagus Pass sign, watching my breath as I exhaled.

A key on mountain climbs is not to go too hard too early. If you "blow up" at the bottom, you're gone. It's better to ride within yourself and start picking people off as the climb goes on. This doesn't mean giving up, because a lot of times the speed is really high at the bottom (in a race) and then it mellows. You have to realize what your capabilities are. Think of climbing as a carpet unrolling; you want to get faster as the climb goes on.

You'll often see riders in the Tour de France let others go away at the bottom of a climb, because they know they can't match the tempo being set. They know that if they hold a comfortable pace, then more than likely they'll be able to get back to the front.

The Kancamagus Highway travels through the heart of the White Mountains of New Hampshire, which cover 87 miles of the state, and extend slightly into Maine. The highest point in the range is Mount Washington, at 6,288 feet. The peak is famous for its extreme weather changes. One of the highest wind velocities ever recorded took place there, at 231 mph!

Our only overnight town in Maine was Fryeburg. It's only about five miles over the border of New Hampshire, but it gave me my thirteenth province or state.

Cattlemen first settled Fryeburg, but it wasn't until after the Revolutionary War that the town began to boom. Preceding the settlement of the town, many famous Indian battles occurred in the area.

Fryeburg is also home to one of the finest prep schools in the country, the Fryeburg Academy. Daniel Webster, a famous orator and politician, taught there at one time.

Admiral Robert Peary also lived in Fryeburg. Peary claimed to be the first American to reach the North Pole.

With only two more meetings before the end of the trip, I thought it was important to attend both of them so I could keep up on the latest happenings. It was also vital to attend because arrangements were being made for transportation and such.

Way back in Everett, Cycle America had swooped up some Pacific Ocean water and placed it in a plastic cylinder. Each week, a new rider got to carry the water across the country (I never got to carry it). When we reached the end, the Pacific Ocean water would be mixed into the Atlantic. It was also decided by Bob Goldberg and Floyd's widow, that Floyd's ashes would be mixed in with the Pacific water and then dumped into the Atlantic.

Upon hearing this, Jersey Joe yelled out, "Floyd's going on a cruise!"

<u>100 Miles to Go!</u>

Date: August 18, day 62
Start: Fryeburg, ME
End: Durham, NH
Riding time: 5:00
Miles: 92
Maximum speed: 35 mph
Average speed: 18.4 mph
Elevation gain: 3,560 feet
Weather: Sunny and cooler, with temperatures in the 60s.

I was an emotional wreck.

With two days to go, this was the start of an emotional roller coaster that would last for several days. Knowing that tomorrow would be the last day of the tour, the route was really insignificant to me.

After only 27 miles I entered New Hampshire again. I tried to stop at every state sign to get a photo. Often I had to wait a few minutes for another rider to come by to take the picture. Since I had gotten my picture taken at the border with Maine, I didn't stop for this one.

A few miles later, I stopped and called my friend Tom in Wisconsin. He had told me to call him often so he could put updates in the local paper. The next day my mom told me that there was another nice article written about me. The headline read, "Palzewic's Amazing Journey Nearly Over."

Ten miles later, there was another photo opportunity for me. Cycle America had painted a sign on the road that read, "100 Miles to the Atlantic." It really hit me hard, as I knew my journey was almost completed. I was glad to finally be done so I could see my family, visit with friends, watch TV, and ***not*** ride my bike 80 miles a day; but, I was also sad because my once-in-a-lifetime journey would be over. At this point, I would say that I was happier that my trip would be done, though.

On this day we stayed in Durham, New Hampshire, home to the University of New Hampshire; it's really beautiful. Durham was named for Durham, England. Durham was important during the American Revolution.

I strolled around the campus and then checked my email for the last time. The university had a huge computer lab and I was able to sit there for an hour. I remember getting quite emotional writing. People wouldn't hear from me now until I got home a few days later.

This night Cycle America had the awards banquet for us. We each got a plaque from the company and Greg Walsh said a little about each rider; it was really nice.

It was also our last awards night. Bob Goldberg (with Floyd) gave me a signed picture from the NBA's all-time leader in wins, Lenny Wilkins. He knows him personally. Bob also stood up and said that I and three other young riders on the tour, were four of the finest young people he had ever had the privilege of knowing. I will remember that comment for the rest of my life. We all left the banquet in tears.

<u>The Atlantic Ocean!</u>

Date: August 19, day 63
Start: Durham, NH
End: Gloucester, MA
Riding time: 3:30
Miles: 62
Maximum speed: 32 mph
Average speed: 17.7 mph
Elevation gain: 2,350 feet
Weather: Mostly sunny and warm, with temperatures in the 70s.

This was both the saddest and happiest day of my life.

After working so hard for nine weeks, I was physically and mentally ready to be done...my body and mind were shot. I just wanted to pack up my bike, board the plane, and get home...until I began riding.

For the first ten miles, I went as slow as possible. I just didn't want it to end. A wave of emotion swept over me and I cried for an hour straight. I don't consider myself an overly emotional person, so I was a bit surprised at how it affected me. It took me the whole summer to realize what I had done. Just like that rainy day in South Dakota, this day has changed my life forever.

For the first time on the trip, I wasn't focused on my speed, license plates, and my destination for the day...or that stupid computer. I was focused on riding as slow as possible and reminiscing about the trials and tribulations of seeing the U.S. from the seat of a bicycle. It has a way of changing a person.

As other riders passed me, I was in no frame of mind to say very much. I pride myself on being easy to talk to, but on this day, I didn't have a clue what to say. Somehow they knew that I couldn't talk with them.

Slowly as the miles ticked by, my tears of sadness turned into ones of joy. I soon was riding faster and wanting it to all end.

Our last lunch spot was very festive. With the short mileage, most all the riders got there within an hour of each other. Cycle America had wanted all of us to get to Gloucester as soon as possible, so we could make arrangements to end the tour.

I reached Gloucester at about 11 a.m. There was a waterfront festival going on, but I still managed to get a view of the Atlantic Ocean. It was everything I expected…and more.

Samuel Champlain first mapped out Gloucester and colonists from England settled the site. It was named for Gloucester, England. Today it thrives as a maritime and fishing center. Since the area was settled, it's estimated that 10,000 fishermen have lost their lives at sea. The Fishermen's Memorial, a bronze statue facing the harbor, honors those who died. Gloucester was the backdrop for "The Perfect Storm," a movie starring George Clooney.

When I finally crossed that finish line, I knew beyond a doubt, that it was the happiest day of my life. Another wave of emotion swept over me and I cried again! Other riders came up to me and tried to comfort me, but it didn't work. It just made me cry harder.

It wasn't something I immediately thought about when crossing the finish line, but I also managed to successfully complete my goal of riding every mile of Coast-to-Coast 2000. I felt that if I hadn't ridden every mile of the tour, I would regret it for the rest of my life.

Even though it was my goal to ride every mile of the tour, I fault no one for not doing the same. It all could have changed at the drop of a hat, and it almost did. If things hadn't happened precisely as they did, I wouldn't have been able to do it. There were a couple of riders on Coast-to-Coast 2000 that were equal to me (or better) in terms of cycling, but they didn't ride every mile because luck wasn't on their side.

What if that storm hadn't chased me to Pierre? Little things like that make me realize how precious each situation was. There were about a dozen of us who rode every mile on the trip, and we were a very stubborn group. I think because of my German background, it would have been the hardest thing in the world for me to raise my hand to get a lift from the van. There was absolutely no way that I would allow that to happen. I hope I didn't offend anyone by my stubborn attitude.

For the next couple of hours, other riders slowly came in. It was a great feeling to see them all finish. There is one rider I will remember that day and the joy he went through when he crossed the line.

I had finished ahead of Jim Wermerskirchen by about an hour, so I knew that his family had come from Minnesota to Gloucester to surprise him. Jim had no idea they would be there. When he finished, he ended up riding right by them. It was not until he stopped and looked again that he realized who they were! It was one of the neatest things I've ever seen in my life. They all hugged, kissed, and cried. A third wave of emotions hit me…you guessed it…I cried again!

After all the riders finished (and I was done crying), Cycle America had set up a ceremony in the Atlantic Ocean for us to dip our front tires. If you recall, we started the trip by dipping our back tires in the Pacific.

The streets were crammed with traffic from the waterfront festival, so the police did us a favor. They stopped traffic long enough so we could get to the ocean and complete our journey. I guess I was all cried out, because I kept my composure this time. I think I was more concerned about not getting my Lemond steel frame wet with salt water.

It sure was an unusual way of connecting the continent.

It was also time to dump the Pacific Ocean (and Floyd) water into the Atlantic. It meant so much to her, that Beth Clark (Floyd's widow) was there to watch it all.

With that, our coast-to-coast journey was completed…except for one thing…a party!

After a quick shower, I changed into my first set of "normal" clothes in a long time. I was so used to wearing t-shirts and shorts that I forgot what it felt like to wear anything different.

Cycle America bussed us to John Harvard's in Boston for the special occasion. It was a grand occasion for all. It was also a time to say good-bye for the last time. It was definitely a weird feeling having to do that, because these were the people I had spent the last nine weeks of my life with.

Before taking the Amtrak out to Washington, I had made arrangements to stay with some friends in Boston after the tour ended.

A teacher friend of mine from the school where I teach has two kids who live out there. It was a big burden off my mind not having to worry about finding a room.

Another rider and his wife actually stayed with us, too. At John Harvard's, Jeff Bucher was joined by his wife, Claire. Jeff was spending most of the party on the phone looking for a motel, but to no avail. He came up to my friends and asked if they knew of a motel in the area, since he was having trouble finding one. They took one look at each other, and offered to let them stay in their apartment! They really didn't even know us, but they were willing to help us out in a time of need.

<u>The Day After</u>

The morning after Lance Armstrong won his first Tour de France, he woke up and said to his wife, "Oh my God. I won the Tour de France."

His wife chuckled, "No way!"

That's how I felt the day after completing my cross-country tour. I wasn't sure what I had just done.

My friends and I spent the next two days relaxing and touring the Boston area. We took in a play called "Shear Madness" and a Red Sox game. It was the first time I had seen Fenway Park, but the fourth time I'd seen the play. I had seen it the other three times in Washington D.C. at the Kennedy Center, where I take a group of sixth graders every year (I've since seen it one more time).

On Monday August 21, 2000, my bike and I headed back to Milwaukee via airplane. After finishing in Gloucester, I had my bike boxed up.

<u>The Aftermath</u>

When I landed in Milwaukee my parents were waiting for me. I shook my dad's hand and gave my mom a hug. It was only the second time I had seen them in ten weeks, so it was an emotional time for them and me. Their support and confidence in me helped me make it through the summer.

The trip back to Michigan took about three and one-half hours. We stopped at a friend's house on the way home, but I quickly fell asleep on the floor. I guess the summer had finally caught up with me.

Tour riders are usually given one or two days off during the three-week stage race. You would think that the riders would spend their day off relaxing and doing absolutely nothing...wrong! It's funny how the body works when it's put to the test.

When racing full bore, your body produces more endorphins and adrenaline than normal. If you suddenly stop the high intensity, the production of these hormones ceases, and the body goes into shock. To combat this, riders often go for a two or three-hour ride on their rest day. It's not to stay in shape or lose weight, but to keep the production of those hormones going strong. I think that would explain why I was always tired on our rest days and the day after. Maybe if I had gone out for a little spin it would have changed things.

We got home early in the morning and I went straight to bed. Later the same morning I sat and reminisced with my parents about the summer. I read them parts of my journal and called friends. I even went for a short ride to see what it felt like. I spent a few days in Michigan before leaving with my cat and bike for Rhinelander.

Before I left, though, I had to fix the two flat tires on my car!

<u>Life After the Trip</u>

Home again!

After eleven long weeks, I finally returned to Rhinelander. It was a strange feeling entering my house again. It had seemed like I just left, but I knew I hadn't.

When people ask me about my summer, I tell them that it was the best summer and vacation of my life, but it also didn't feel like I had any time off. I had left one week after school ended, and got home just one week before it started again. So as soon as the ride ended and I got back to Rhinelander, my mind shifted to school…and I got very scared! I usually spend a large portion of time in August getting my classroom and lessons all ready to go for the first day of class, but not this year. I think it took me half the year to feel comfortable.

Just like Greg Walsh told us, it was definitely hard returning to normality. It's hard to understand it unless you've done something like this yourself. Even though rewarding and fun, the trip became like a job to me. I had the same routine every day…eat, sleep, and ride, eat, sleep, and ride. When that routine was taken away, it was hard to readjust to the real world.

I missed the people, their stories, the scenery, my license plate game, and having a destination; I missed the challenge, the 112-degree day, the mountains, the yellow arrows, and playing with my computer for five hours; I missed sweating, the mosquitoes, the bunk house, the wheat and soy bean fields, and the logging trucks; I missed Washtucna, checking my email, calling home, the history, and puking in South Dakota; I missed the late-night trains and fireworks exploding in my ear, unloading the Penske, and riding in the rain; I missed the bad water, Cottonwood, urinating in the middle of nowhere, and eating as much as I wanted; I missed the ocean, eating ice cream, freezing to death, going 50 mph, and being in great shape; I missed the Rainbow Family, writing postcards, Devils Tower, the buffalo dung, and the 35 miles of downhill; I missed the huckleberries, getting up at 5:00 a.m., the Cycle America staff, the picnic in Menasha, and the ferry ride over Lake Michigan; I missed Canada, changing a flat, crying, cattle grates, and taking a picture at each state sign; I missed the seven-hour day in South Dakota, my farmer's tan, and stopping in the most desolate place in the world to look around me; I missed the bike paths, sleeping on a gym floor, and the steam bath in Lolo Hot Springs; I missed Needles Highway, the exhilaration of ending in Gloucester, Jersey Joe, and Bobby Kennedy; heck, I even missed Sid's snoring; but most of all, I missed riding my bike.

I had definitely been living in a fantasy world for the last eleven weeks, and now I was expected to come back down to earth and live as usual.

There was another potential problem I faced...eating too much. My body changed on the trip, but I didn't lose any weight. The muscles in my legs became more defined and sleek, and my upper body sort of melted away. I was used to eating whatever I wanted at any time of the day, and now I couldn't do that. As I said earlier, I didn't eat very well on the trip. I ate a lot of junk, but I suppose it didn't really matter.

I've heard that your stomach expands the more you eat, and it takes some time for that to shrink back down to size when you're not eating as much. It really wasn't as much a problem as I thought it would be, though. I just had to be careful for a while and realize that I couldn't eat 6,000 calories or more a day and get away with it. I've managed to maintain my weight within five pounds.

Had I been asked halfway through the trip if I'd do it again, I probably would have said no. But now, there's no doubt in my mind that I would. Having that feeling of finishing was without a doubt, the best feeling I've ***ever*** experienced in my life.

I have thought about Coast-to-Coast 2000 ***every*** day since I've returned. It has made me a better person. I don't let little things bother me as much and realize that life, just like my trip, has to be taken in segments, day by day, hour by hour, and maybe even minute by minute. I also don't give up as easily anymore. When faced with a hard situation, I simply think back to that rainy day in South Dakota, and realize that things aren't so bad.

As Lance Armstrong has said, "I now have only good days and great days."

It's also made me a better teacher. I'm able to tell my students about the historical importance of different areas of the country and relate stories to them. A lot of my students come from divorced backgrounds (as do a lot of others) and my trip has helped me relate to their situation better. I tell them that if things were meant to be easy, life wouldn't be a challenge. As my mom always told me, "things happen for a reason." Some people were dealt a difficult hand, but if they can see the hardships I went through, maybe it will help show them that there's hope. I don't think God ever gives a person more than he can handle.

I'm also more adventurous now. Before, I was afraid to fly (even though I did) or do much of anything, but traveling across the country on a bike changed all that. Each new situation I was faced with, forced me to deal with it in a calm and thoughtful manner. I would consider trying almost anything now.

If there's anything negative that's come about from the trip, maybe I'm a bit more critical of my students and other people now. After going through this trip, I don't have as much patience with some people. I think to myself, "Darn it. If I can pedal my bike for seven hours, in 50-degree, rainy weather, into a 25-mph headwind, all after spending time in the hospital, you can do that math problem."

The Final Stats

Days on the trip: 63
Days of riding: 54
Days off: 8
Total Miles: 4,284
Average miles per day: 79.3
Longest riding day in miles: 108
Shortest riding day in miles: 49
Total riding time: 235:53
Average riding time per day: 4:22
Longest riding day in time: 6:50
Shortest riding day in time: 2:30
Maximum speed: 57 mph
Overall average speed: 18.2 mph
Fastest average speed in a day: 20.8 mph
Slowest average speed in a day: 13.9 mph
Total elevation gained (the amount of feet going uphill): 158,490 feet
Average elevation gained per day: 2,935 feet
Most elevation gained in a day: 8,400 feet
Least elevation gained in a day: 810 feet
Flat tires: 10
Estimated calories consumed: 351,000
Estimated pedal reps: 1,237,806
Ferryboat rides: 4
Provinces or states ridden through: 14
Oceans touched: 2
Great Lakes seen: 4
Friends made: too many to count
Hours of crying: 3

<u>Epilogue</u>

I hope by reading this book, you were in fact, able to live vicariously through me on my journey. I hope it has inspired you to set your goals high, and realize that the human body and mind can do amazing things when put to the test.

Two years after completing my coast-to-coast bike trip, I am still riding my bike, cross-country skiing, teaching the 6th grade, crying, watching "Little House on the Prairie," and most importantly, thinking about my incredible summer of 2000.

Richard Palzewic

<u>Index</u>

Adirondack State Park, 162
altimeter, 31
Amish, 138
Amtrak, 10, 17, 180
Armstrong, Lance, v, 32, 33,
    52, 54, 55, 69, 79, 104, 106,
    110, 111, 116, 128, 129,
    138, 146, 147, 148, 153,
    182, 185
Artigas, Jose, 116
Aruba, 8
Atlantic Ocean, 13, 41, 99,
    100, 115, 141, 157, 175,
    176, 178, 179, 180
Badlands, 86, 87, 95
Banks, Murray, 108
Bates Battlesite, 68
Ben and Jerry's, 171
bicycle equipment
    clothing, 39, 40
bicycle maintenance
    broken spokes, 27, 28, 51,
        101
    changing a flat, 22, 184
    cleaning, 121
    derailleur, 28
bicycle safety, vii
    helmet use, 14, 149
    traffic, 26, 27, 45, 72, 137,
        154, 157, 162, 168, 170,
        180
    weather, 4, 9, 17, 24, 39, 40,
        47, 50, 52, 60, 64, 80,
        104, 105, 145, 175, 186

Big Hole Battlefield, 42
bike paths, 124, 156, 185
Black Hills, 78, 80, 81, 82, 87
camping, 3, 11
Canada, 29, 125, 143, 144,
    145, 149, 150, 153, 154,
    158, 160, 164, 165, 170, 184
    Niagara Falls, 150, 151, 153
    Ontario, 29, 135, 143, 144,
        145, 148, 149, 150, 151,
        153, 154, 158, 159, 160,
        161
    Port Dover, 145, 149, 150
    Port Stanley, 148
    West Lorne, 143, 145
cancer, 128, 129
Carleton College, 120
cattle grates, 71, 184
Champlain, Samuel, 162, 179
Christopherson, Ryan, 73
Clark, Beth, v, 24, 151, 175,
    180
Clooney, George, 179
Close Encounters of the Third
    Kind, 75
Continental Divide, 41, 115
Crowheart Butte, 62
Custer State Park, 81
Custer, George Armstrong, 81
Cycle America, v, 2, 3, 4, 5,
    13, 14, 24, 26, 28, 29, 39,
    49, 51, 55, 82, 83, 85, 89,
    105, 106, 107, 115, 119,
    124, 125, 134, 143, 156,

159, 164, 175, 176, 177,
178, 180, 184
luggage transportation, 3
typical day, 4
Cycle America riders
Bucher, Jeff, 8, 13, 18, 35,
39, 181
Clark, Jan, 157
Clark, Sid, 75
Collins, Ed, 14
Goldberg, Bob, 24, 55, 151,
175, 177
Haley, Bob, 65
Hunt, Bob, 169
Oncale, Mark, 141
Paiva, Bob, 48
Patton, Bob, 58
Roehrig, Ted, 71
Stun, Joe, v, 69, 73, 84, 112,
157, 175, 185
Wermerskirchen, Jim, 180
cycling tactics or terms
blocking, 111
bonking, 107, 108
drafting, 110
mountain goat, 61
saddle sores, 131
cycling techniques
aerodynamics, 16, 57, 116
climbing, 16, 31, 33, 56, 69,
70, 75, 90, 92, 117, 170,
174
dealing with dogs, 118, 119
descending, 17, 27, 33, 62,
153
gearing, 56, 57
gravel riding, 44, 45, 46, 50,
132
railroad tracks, 21, 153
riding in the rain, 14, 62,
104, 140, 142, 184
saddle height, 53
sprinting, 148
Deception Falls, 16
dehydration, 64, 65, 70, 80
Devils Tower, 74, 75, 76, 78,
120, 184
Earthquake Lake, 49, 51
eating, 8, 51, 88, 89, 90, 130,
132, 146, 153, 184, 185
effects of the trip, 140
Embargo Act, 170
Erie Canal, 156
European cycling, 33
Father DeSmet, 112
fear, 6, 17
Fenway Park, 182
Fisher Railroad Bridge, 172
Flintstone Campground, 81
Floyd, v, 24, 25, 151, 175, 177,
180
Fourth of July, 27, 60, 62, 63,
78
Fryeburg Academy, 175
Grand Coulee Dam, 20
Grand Teton, 53, 58
Great Depression, 83, 87
Great Lakes, 134, 144, 147,
154, 156, 187
Erie, 98, 145, 147, 149, 151
Huron, 134, 139
Michigan 131, 133, 134, 184

Ontario, 151, 154, 158, 159, 160, 161
Superior, 134, 154
Gretsky, Wayne, 54
Hell's Canyon, 81
Highline Canal, 18
Hoosiers, 137
huckleberries, 39, 184
hypothermia, 13, 33, 62, 105
Idaho, 12, 29, 30, 31, 38, 47, 53, 62, 64
Ashton, 53, 55, 56
Lewiston, 26
Lowell, 29, 30, 31
James, Jesse, 120
Jewel Cave, 80, 94
Jordan, Michael, 54
Kaeser, Tom, v, 10, 108, 176
Kancamagus Highway, 174
Kennedy, Bobby, v, 18, 93, 185
La Guerre d' Independence, 158
lacrosse, 164, 165, 166
lactic acid, 116, 117
Lake Champlain, 168
laundry, 35, 39, 55, 85
Lewis and Clark, 19, 26, 31, 35, 36, 39, 41, 46, 65
license plate game, 114, 184
Little House on the Prairie, 112, 125, 189
Lombardi, Vince, 68
Mackinac Bridge, 136, 142
Maine, 174, 175, 176
Fryeburg, 174, 175, 176
Mall of America, 121

Mammoth Cave, 80
Massachusetts, vii, 100
Boston, 180, 182
Gloucester, vii, 88, 100, 157, 178, 179, 180, 182, 185
maximum heart rate, 146, 147
meals, 3
metric system, 143
Michigan, v, 1, 10, 15, 64, 90, 97, 108, 118, 124, 131, 133, 134, 135, 136, 137, 138, 139, 141, 143, 144, 183, 184, 199
Farwell, 136, 138
Frankenmuth, 138, 139, 140
Ludington, 134
Marine City, 143
Menominee, 15
Reed City, 137
Richmond, 140, 142, 143
Scottville, 134, 136
Stephenson, 137
Upper Peninsula, 142, 199
Wallace, v, 199
Minnesota, 2, 14, 96, 103, 115, 116, 119, 120, 124, 180
Cannon Falls, 124, 125
Hutchinson, 118, 119, 120
Madison, 115
Minneapolis, 121
Montevideo, 115, 116, 118
Northfield, 120, 124
Red Wing, 124
Minolta Tower, 153

Montana, 12, 31, 35, 37, 38,
    39, 42, 44, 46, 47, 48, 51,
    64, 92, 93, 154, 157
  Corvallis, 39
  Darby, 38, 39, 41
  Dillon, 44, 46, 47
  Ennis, 47, 48, 49
  Jackson, 41, 42, 44,
  Lolo Hot Springs, 31, 35,
    38, 185
  Nevada City, 47
  Virginia City, 47
  West Yellowstone, 49, 51,
    53, 93
  Wisdom, 42
Mount Mansfield, 170
Mount Marcy, 162
Mount Rushmore, 82, 83
Mount Washington, 175
mountain passes
  Big Hole, 45, 46
  Chief Joseph, 41
  Kancamagus, 174
  L'Alpe d' Huez, 16
  Lolo, 31, 34, 157
  Lost Trail, 41, 157
  Powder River, 69, 70
  Sestrieres, 32
  Stevens, 14, 16, 17, 19, 31,
    92
  Teton, 56, 57, 93
  Togwatee, 60, 61, 62
moutain ranges
  Adirondack, 162
  Appalachian, 168
  Big Horn, 68, 69
  Bitterroot, 38, 39, 92, 154

  Cascade, 14, 29
  Gravely, 47
  Green, 168
  Madison, 47
  Teton, 55, 56, 57, 61, 93
  White, 174
Murwin, Don, 15
Native Americans, 38, 81
  Algonquian, 174
  Arapahoe, 68
  Chief Joseph, 41, 42
  Chief Moses, 20
  Crazy Horse, 81, 83
  Kancamagus, 174
  Nez Perce, 41, 42
  Shoshones, 69
  Sioux, 81
Needles Highway, 82, 185
New Hampshire, 172, 173,
    174, 175, 176, 177
  Durham, 176, 177, 178
  Littleton, 172, 173, 174
New York, 83, 114, 152, 156,
    158, 159, 160, 161, 162,
    163, 164, 168, 169
  Albion, 153, 156
  Lake Placid, 164, 165, 168
  Mexico, 158, 159, 160
  New York City, 156
  Rochester, 156
  Sackets Harbor, 160, 161
  Sodus, 156, 158, 159
  Sodus Point, 159
  Star Lake, 162, 163, 164
  Watertown, 114, 160, 161,
    162
Norski Nook, 126

Northern Lights, 173
Pacific Ocean, 13, 31, 41, 115,
    175, 180
Peary, Robert, 175
Penske, 159, 184
praying, 44, 108
preparation
    mental, 7, 32
    packing, 40
    physical, 6, 7, 70, 169
    weather, 4, 9, 39, 40, 60, 64
professional cycling races
    Championship of Zurich, 52
    Paris-Roubaix, 50, 51, 111,
        112, 150
    San Sebastian, 52
    Tour de France, vii, 16, 17,
        31, 32, 33, 53, 55, 57, 61,
        69, 78, 106, 110, 116,
        129, 138, 148, 155, 174,
        182
    Tour of Spain, 129
professional cyclists
    Bauer, Steve, 150
    Bortolami, Gianluca, 111,
        112
    Indurain, Miguel, 32, 155
    Jemison, Marty, 15
    Kelly, Sean, 57
    Lemond, Greg, 33, 57
    Merckx, Eddy, 53, 54, 55,
        61, 79
    Museeuw, Johann, 111, 112
    Riis, Bjarne, 33
    Rooy, Teho de, 51
    Tafi, Andrea, 111, 112
    Ullrich, Jan, 32, 116

PSI, 45, 46
RAGBRAI, 1
Rainbow Bridge, 154
Rainbow Family, 42, 184
red-rock formations, 64, 66
resting heart rate, 154, 155
Revolutionary War, 173, 175
riding every mile, 108, 141,
    179
rivers
    Badwater, 66
    Beaverhead, 46
    Chippewa, 116
    Columbia, 19
    Connecticut, 172
    Hudson, 156
    Lamoille, 172
    Little Big Horn, 81
    Madison, 48, 51
    Minnesota, 116
    Mississippi, 125
    Missouri, 102, 104
    Niagara, 151, 154
    Snake, 27
    St. Claire, 143
    St. Lawrence, 125
    Wisconsin, 128
road rash, 168
Rudolph, Wilma, 109
Rushmore, Charles E., 83
Scriba, George, 158
shaving your legs, 168
Smuggler's Notch, 170
South Dakota, 77, 78, 80, 81,
    82, 84, 85, 86, 87, 94, 95,
    101, 102, 103, 105, 106,

108, 112, 114, 140, 145,
161, 178, 184, 185
Bryant, 114
Cottonwood, 87, 95, 184
Custer, 80, 81, 82
DeSmet, 110, 112, 113
Fort Pierre, 101, 102, 104
Interior, 84, 85, 86
Miller, 104, 105, 107, 110
Philip, 86, 87, 101
Pierre, 102, 125, 179
Rapid City, 82, 83, 84, 114
Rapid Creek, 81, 83
Scenic, 84, 85
Wall, 86, 87
Watertown, 113, 114, 115,
161
St. Olaf College, 120
Star Lake Campus, 163
The Perfect Storm, 179
Tour de France Jerseys
Green, 79
Polka Dot, 79
White, 79
Yellow, 79
Trapper Peak, 38
types of bicycles
mountain, 49
recumbent, 48, 140
road, 121, 122
tandem, 133
Underground Railroad, 158
University of New Hampshire,
177
University of Vermont, 168
valleys
Bitterroot, 38, 39, 154

Madison, 47
Vermont, 162, 168, 170, 172
Burlington, 168, 170, 171
South Peachman, 172
Stowe, 170, 171, 172
Von Trapp family, 171
Wall Drug, 87
Walsh, Greg, 3, 5, 17, 20, 22,
58, 143, 157, 177, 184
War of 1812, 151, 160, 161,
168
Washington, vii, 10, 12, 14,
18, 19, 21, 22, 27, 29, 44,
55, 92, 130, 139, 180, 182
Clarkston, 26, 29
Everett, vii, 10, 13, 24, 175
Leavenworth, 18, 139
Moses Lake, 19, 20, 21
Seattle, 13, 24, 55
Skykomish, 13, 14, 15, 16,
76
Washtucna, 21, 22, 23, 26,
65, 184
Wenatchee, 16, 18, 19
Webster, Daniel, 175
Welland Canal, 150
West Indies, 158
Whiteface Mountain, 168
Wilder, Laura Ingalls, 112, 125
Wilkins, Lenny, 177
Wind River Canyon, 66
Winter Olympics, 164, 165
Wisconsin, v, 10, 21, 26, 29,
48, 72, 80, 82, 87, 90, 97,
108, 119, 123, 124, 125,
127, 128, 130, 131, 162,
173, 176, 199

Green Bay, 131, 132
Manitowoc, 131, 133, 134
Marinette, 10
Menasha, 97, 128, 131, 132, 133, 141, 184
Milwaukee, 10, 88, 125, 182, 183
Osseo, 125, 126, 127, 128
Pepin, 124, 125, 126, 127, 128
Rhinelander, v, 10, 38, 47, 118, 128, 130, 183, 184, 199
Wisconsin Rapids, 128, 130, 131
Woods, Tiger, 54

Wyoming, 37, 53, 55, 56, 57, 59, 62, 63, 64, 65, 66, 67, 68, 70, 72, 73, 74, 77, 78, 93, 173
Buffalo, 68, 70, 72
Devils Tower, 74, 75, 76, 78, 120, 184
Dubois, 60, 62, 64
Gillette, 72, 73, 74
Jackson, 55, 56, 57, 58, 60
New Castle, 78, 80
Riverton, 64, 65, 66
Ten Sleep, 68
Thermopolis, 66
Worland, 66, 67, 68
Yellowstone National Park, 58
Yoopers, 136, 137

About the Author

Richard Palzewic grew up in the rural community of Wallace in the Upper Peninsula of Michigan with his parents and six sisters (a topic for another book). He graduated from Northern Michigan University in 1995 with a B.S. degree in elementary education. Richard is currently teaching and coaching in Rhinelander, Wisconsin, and completing course work on his Master's Degree. In his spare time, he likes to bike and cross-country ski. He biked across the country in the summer of 2000, and has aspirations of competing in the Race Across America (RAAM) during the summer of 2004. Richard has also participated in North America's largest cross-country ski race, the American Birkebeiner, four times.